tempus fugit...

It's About Time
Time Saving Tips
for Every Day
— Home & Away —

by
Schar Ward

author of **DISCARDED**
Coming Clean
Dirty Little Secrets of a Professional Housecleaner

Book Peddlers
Minnetonka, MN

Cover production by Pettit Network Inc.
Cover design by Amy Kirkpatrick

ISBN 1-931863-28-8
(new ISBN 13: 978-1931-86328-5)

copyright© 2006 Schar Ward

Publisher's Cataloging-in-Publication
(Provided by Quality Books, Inc.)

Ward, Schar.
  It's about time : time saving tips for every day, home
& away / by Schar Ward.
  p.cm
  Includes bibliographical reference and index.
  ISBN-13: 978-1-931863-28-5
  ISBN-10: 1-931863-28-8

  1. Home economics. 2. Time management. I. Title.

TX158.W37 2006   640'.43
                      QBI05-600131

BOOK PEDDLERS
15245 Minnetonka Blvd • Minnetonka, MN 55345
952-912-0036 • fax 952-912-0105
www.bookpeddlers.com • info@bookpeddlers.com

printed in the USA

06 07 08 09 10   5 4 3 2 1

FOREWORD

Well, it's about time! Someone has put together a great collection of time saving tips that can really make a difference.

I'm not sure when I started *running out of time.* It seems to be one of those things that crept up on me. I don't think it was in or after college. Life was a bit simpler then—or is this only hindsight? I think it was when the kids came along and I fell into my own business of writing and self-publishing my parenting and household hints books. Divorce added a whole new dimension of trying to do it all myself.

Now my children are adults and I'm a grandparent. I can leave the house in the morning and it looks the same when I come home. It took a lot of years to reach this point. More than I had thought. But you get in the habit of looking for ways to be efficient and save time when you feel you have little of it and those habits don't go away. I may have more these days but in other ways I'm aware that I have less so every shortcut is still a welcome addition to my life. And hopefully these will be to yours!

— *Vicki Lansky*

Table of Contents

Technology To the Rescue

Getting From Here to There

introduction

I'll bet when you opened this book you thought I was going to start by teaching you time management. You know, things like setting priorities, listing your goals and having a plan. Well, I am not going to do that because most of the time, it does not work.

A few years ago time management professionals approached working parents with a matter–of–fact, can–do attitude. Their message was, if you just try harder and follow a few simple organizational principles, everything would fall into place and you wouldn't stumble into bed each night exhausted. Interestingly enough, I don't think they are teaching this idea anymore. I am not sure why, but I suspect they got married, had children, and became working parents themselves.

I am a professional house cleaner and over the years I have observed my clients, trying all manner of things so they could become more efficient and fit more things into their house and their day. I have watched as they bought and read (at least I think they read them) books on creating more time, controlling your time and managing your time. They made lists they could not find, and set goals they could not keep. They bought all kinds of organizers they did not use and the organizers took up more room than the things they were trying to organize! With each new plan that failed they became more frustrated.

I could see plainly what their problem was—they just had too much stuff and were trying to fit an eighteen hour schedule into an eight hour day. You just can't do it!

Now I am not suggesting that you just give up and admit defeat, but I do think it is important not to set unreal expectations for yourself. People have too much information to absorb. We have more numbers to remember, more places to go and things to do, our minds are on overload, and we still keep doing more!

So, what I want to teach you is how to pare down, slow down and enjoy life. I will show you how to build and furnish your home to make life easier, cleaning supplies that will cut your cleaning time and storage ideas that will get you more organized. Here are tips that will save you a minute here and a minute there. Shortcuts that will get the job done fast and advice that will save you time down the road.

Many of the hints in this book have been handed down to me by my family and friends. Some from seminar participants and a lot I learned on my own by having a professional maid service for thirty years.

I can't promise you stress free living or make you the most organized person on the planet, but I can promise you that after reading this book and using just a few of my suggestions, you will have more time to work on these things. *And isn't it about time!*

Schar Ward

I am definitely going to take a course on time management...just as soon as I can work it into my schedule.
—Louis E. Boone

Timing is Everything

Good health means good timing-from when you rise and shine to when you eat, work and exercise. You can stay in step with your body clock by knowing a little about its natural peaks and troughs. The following, according to an article in *SHAPE* magazine, describes the best time of the day to engage in various mental and physical activities.

The Best Time (?) To Do Things

To make decisions is;
• Early morning, between 8 and 8:30 a.m. when anxiety and depression are at their lowest. The worst time is between 2 and 7 p.m. when anxiety and depression are highest. Neutral hours are between 8 p.m. and 2 a.m.

To Count To Ten;
• The three half hours before breakfast, lunch and dinner. Hunger pangs and low blood sugar can make you more irritable and likely to lose your cool during these three "hot spots," so start counting when tempers flare.

To Think Your Most Positive Thoughts;
• Right after you get out of bed. Studies show that unless we're on vacation or have something special to look forward to, most of us experience our most "down" feelings immediately after rising.

3

Moods generally improve throughout the morning and peak by mid-afternoon.

To Read And Reflect
• Between 2 and 4 p.m. when your body temperature starts to drop.

To Feast On Forbidden Fruit;
• If you really must indulge, do so within an hour after you wake up. Calories burn faster and more completely in the morning, because the thyroid is more active and insulin levels are lower. The same meal eaten in the morning is more likely to turn to fat if it's eaten later.

To Take A Caffeine Break;
• Around 3 p.m. Stimulants work best when we're already stimulated; sedatives when we're already sedated. You'll get more of a boost from your caffeine if you drink it at 3 p.m. The typical American wake-up cup of coffee may be based more on mental conditioning than physiological factors.

To Rise And Shine;
• The moment you wake up. Don't linger in bed, as you may use this time to dwell on unpleasant thoughts and start the day tense and nervous.

To Run Your Fastest Mile Or Weight Train;
• In mid to late afternoon, when your body is fastest and strongest.

I'm not sure this is the best advice. It would seem from this information you should do the following:

• Set your alarm for 8:30 a.m. Get up immediately when the alarm goes off and make your cleaning or organizing plan for the day.

Don't lay in bed and make your plan because just thinking about it while there will make you tense and nervous.

• Eat some junk food while making your plan.

• Do not attempt to start cleaning before lunch, because you will be irritable from low blood sugar.

• At 2 p.m. read a good book and at 3 p.m. have a good strong cup of coffee.

• Start cleaning late afternoon, when your body is finally ready for the task.

Oops! The kids are home from school and you must think about dinner so maybe you should wait until tomorrow to start the cleaning. Anyway, this advice says you shouldn't clean three hours before dinner because your blood sugar is once again low and you do not want to be grumpy with your family.

All this time you thought the reason you could not get your house cleaned and organized was your fault, that you were lazy or disorganized. Not true at all—blame it on your *body clock*!

> You may be on the right track,
> but you'll get run over if you just stand there.

Stretch Your Days

Isn't it amazing? You have twenty–four hours everyday to accomplish the things you need or want to do. Some days, you probably feel like you have lived every hour. Other days, the time slips by and you have no idea where it went.

You live in a world where schedules, timetables and deadlines are the bane of your existence. Everyone strives to be organized. You buy books on the subject, attend seminars and even hire people to organize for you. All of these things just take more time. What you need to do is realize what organization is all about. It's not about living by a set of rigid rules. It is about choices.

Organized people have learned to make the right choices for their life. They know what is important to them and have arranged their time and space to focus on these choices.

Take time to reflect on the pace of your life and what is important to you. When you start to feel overwhelmed, it's probably time for some changes.

Here are a few strategy tips to stretch your day, lighten your load and help you to accomplish a bit more.

Get Some Help

You can't do it all. You should be asking for help when your schedule is so full that you are not enjoying life. Take a look around. You'll be surprised at how much help there is for you, if you will just ask.

Driving the kids–driving you nuts? Start a car pool with other parents to save your sanity.

Even the neighbors can help. Maybe you don't know your neighbors too well, but this is a great way to break the ice. For example, one week you cut both lawns and the next week they cut them. Or maybe they have a teenage boy or girl who would be happy to help with lawn work for a small fee. You could also trade off baby–sitting so you could have a night out.

Get up Earlier

When you find yourself running behind in getting the bills paid, laundry done and your plants start to die from lack of water–try getting up a half hour earlier everyday to get a few of these things done. When the rest of the family is sleeping, it is a great time to complete chores. And it may even give you a little more free time in the evening for relaxation.

Stay Up Later

I am not as fond of this as I am getting up earlier, because sometimes family members want to stay up also. The main thing is to stay focused. Make lunches, feed the pets, throw in a load of laundry and even spot clean the house.

Do It Now

Do things as you think about them. Don't procrastinate. This is usually everyone's biggest problem. You need to do it rather than think about it. Follow the waitress rule; never get caught without something in your hands. You carry the coffee cup to the sink and then take the dishes from the dishwasher and put them in the cupboard. You then spot the pitcher you need to put downstairs and before you know it, everything is put away. Simply let your hands lead your feet.

Kids Can Help

No matter how small your children are, there should be a few things they can do to help. Very small children can pick up toys, feed the pets, set the table and make their bed with a little help. I believe that by the time a child is sixteen, they should be able to clean an entire house, do laundry and make a meal. Children need to learn responsibility, and this is a wonderful way to teach them. Children are usually eager to help, just make sure the chore fits the age of the child.

I'm sure you're saying "I can't get them to clean their room, and now you think they will clean the house"? They will, if you approach it in the correct way. Always break the chore down for the child. Don't say, " Go clean your room " say "Please go dust your dresser, or make your bed." Children don't understand time and giving them too much at once overwhelms them—just like it does us. You will free up your time if you teach your children how to help around the house.

Hiring It Out

Hiring someone to clean the house, deliver the groceries, mow the yard or do whatever task you need help with, will give you a much-needed break. It doesn't have to be weekly, it can be occasionally. This may take a little getting used to, because you are used to doing it all, but in the long run it will be well worth it. And a little secret—once you do get used to it; you will wonder what took you so long!

Routine

Take a tip from nursery school teachers who must keep twenty toddlers organized all day. Set a routine and stick to it. Decide in advance what you are going to do and when you are going to do it.

Be Superficial

Learn to skim. Skim your newspapers, magazines and, yes, even some of your books. Every piece of printed material does not have to be read word-for-word. Prioritize your need-to-know of your pages of printed matter.

Just Once

Handle EVERYTHING just once whether it be a problem, a piece of paper, a magazine, a phone call, whatever. Not always easy but definitely faster.

Mini Goals

Set mini goals. Divide any project into bite size pieces and do one thing at a time. Establishing small goals makes it easier to keep track of progress. My Mom always said, "Work by the yard is hard–but by the inch it is a cinch."

Turn Off The Television

This may be the hardest thing to do, but it will make a difference. When you think of how much time is spent watching television, you may decide it is time to make some changes. You could make certain days of the week TV free. And please turn it off during dinner. The extra time can be spent with friends or hobbies, or just daydreaming.

Many swear by Tivo's programing abilities to control their TV watching and to eliminate watching commericals.

A Daily Planner

Many people find they cannot get along without the help of their daily planner. And while I am not a big advocate of lists, this is one tool that can be very helpful. A good daily planner:
- is both a calendar and a notebook.
- should be small enough to carry with you (in your purse or bag).
- has a section for phone numbers and addresses.
- should be big enough to hold appointments and lists—assuming lists work for you.

You don't have to buy the most expensive one in the store. You can find one for around ten or fifteen dollars. A planner helps you keep things together. It reduces all those Post-it Notes you put everywhere. You can look at your planner in the evening and envision your next day.

> Chewing gum proves that motion
> doesn't always mean progress.

How to Eke Out Just a FEW More Minutes...

Just Say No!
The biggest time saver you can have is learning to say 'no.' Being interrupted when doing something is not only irritating but a big deterrent in accomplishing your goals.

Click Point
When choosing a pen, select one with a click–point that requires only one hand to use—without removing, storing and replacing a cap.

Save a Second
When done using the toothpaste, screw on the cap right away (this might save arguments with your mate) wipe your shoes before entering the house; change out of good clothing before you make dinner and clean up spills as they happen.

Too Hot–Too Cold
Set your shower to the desired temperature and put a dot of nail polish on the knob and the wall behind it. For the perfect shower simply line up the dots. No more wasting time adjusting the water.

Unplanned Time
Use unplanned time such as the doctor's waiting room to answer letters or balance your check book.

Take A Back Seat
Put clothes that need to go to the cleaners and library books that have to be returned in the back seat of your car. They'll be ready whenever you are near where they need to be dropped off.

Trek Trip

When serving food or drinks in any room other than the kitchen, use a tray. You will save trips back and forth when serving and cleaning up.

Top Drawer

Store frequently used items in top drawers. No explanation needed here.

Size Wise

Keep a list in your wallet of each family member's clothing sizes, color preferences and brand choices. This eliminates standing in line to exchange something that didn't meet expectations.

Dust Less

Keep your windows closed unless you are airing out your house especially in the spring when the trees are budding. That green stuff you find on your dust cloth is pollen and it wreaks havoc with your nose. I always have to laugh when I go to clean a home and the lady of the house is complaining about allergies and making sure I don't use any chemicals and her windows are wide open letting in all kinds of pollutants.

Be Prepared

Stockpile what you can in terms of dollars and space. A "present" closet for those inevitable last minute needed gifts; TP on sale; extra school supplies in the fall. It saves many a trip.

Stashing

Before you store away anything in a box, label the contents as specifically as possible. Also, ask yourself, if I were looking for "this," where would I look. Then put it THERE!

Emergency Keys

Leave an extra set of house keys with a trusty neighbor. Not only can you get in if you lose your own set (or lock yourself out) but your neighbor has access in case of an emergency. The same thing can work for car keys, especially if you don't have other family members nearby who can keep a spare set with them.

Pill People

If you have a large variety of pills or vitamins you take on a daily basis, buy one or two containers of a daily pill compartment holder. This saves you from opening the six or more bottles you have to go through each day.

Decide What You Want Before You Look For It

You'll navigate the mall or a store more efficiently if you're guided by a shopping list that includes everything you want and need, whether it is a comfortable pair of shoes or a red shirt to go with your black pants.

Make Decisions Once

Wear the same jewelry with the same outfit; eat meat loaf every Tuesday; always buy white roses. Boring you say? Maybe. But it is things like this that can make you a woman with time on her hands.

Shop At Your Favorite Store

Shopping at your favorite store, especially when grocery shopping, saves a lot of time. You know where everything is and you won't waste time figuring out the layout. You will also save energy because you will almost certainly find something you like.

Call Ahead

Before you make a trip to the store for a particular item, especially a book, call first to see if it is in stock. The clerk can hold it for you at the front desk. No searching; no lost time.

Travel Time

Avoid the bank and post office during peak times such as Fridays, the first of the month, the hours between noon and one p.m. and around five o'clock.

Cutting Time

Buy several pairs of scissors and keep them in every room. Then you can snip tags, clip coupons and open boxes without spending time looking for the scissors. I found a small fold–up pair that I carry in my purse. They have proven invaluable. Just remember to remove them when going on an airplane.

Return To Sender

Carry return-address stickers in your day planner or wallet. Whenever you need to fill out a form it's simple. This is especially good when you drop off film or put a CD in the mail.

Handy Gifts

Take advantage of seasonal holiday clearances to stock a gift shelf. Often items included in a particular holiday clearance are suitable for any gift–giving occasion. When you keep a gift box stocked with gifts you always have them on hand, which will save you both time and money.

Check, Please

When eating out, ask for the check before you finish the meal.

Geographical Economy
Practice geographical economy; arrange errands in geographical order. Write your to-do list on a Post–It and place the Post–It Note on the dashboard of your car.

Forward Thinking
Do forward thinking exercises. Anticipate roadblocks and other such problems. If you are going to make a speech or just a public comment, know how you will end as well as start.

Put It Back
Always put things back where you found them, whether it is tools or kitchen equipment. Knowing where things are located helps you move faster. The old saying, *"A place for everything and everything in it's place,"* has been around for a long time and for good reason. This simple rule works.

Automat
Use self-dispensing pet food dishes for both water and dry food and you'll save yourself lots of time tending your animal(s).

Garbage Mail
Open your mail over the garbage can or recycle bin. Then you will need to handle most of it only once.

Teen Cooks
Talk your teenager into preparing a dinner for the family one night each week. Not only is this great practice for when they are on their own, but you will have one less meal to think about.

Calendar Girl
When you get your new calendar, immediately transfer all recurring due dates and events such as birthdays, anniversaries and tax payments, to it. You can do this while watching television. (Or get in sync with your computer's calendar which will do this for you.)

Bag-A-Bag

To make it easy to find items in your purse, have a separate colorful small bag for cosmetics, food items, bits of needed paper and pills, etc. When you need a pill, you will know to reach for the red bag. Saves a lot of time rummaging around in your purse.

New Address

A quick way to let your friends and relatives know your new address is to send them a note and enclose an address label. They can stick the label in their address book. Quicker for you and them!

Speaking Of Address Books

When entering names in your address book, enter the names in ink, but the phone numbers, addresses and e-mail addresses in pencil. Then you can erase when needed. It keeps your address book looking nicer.

Invitations And Directions

Attach envelopes to your large calendar, one for each month. When invitations to events come in, mark the event on the calendar and place the invitation in the envelope. Usually the invitations have the directions to the party and this will save you time searching for the directions at a later date.

Mulch More

Mulch your garden plants (and even your window boxes with spaghum moss) and you will spend less time watering.

Time may be a great healer, but it's a lousy beautician.

And What About You?

Making time for yourself is often the hardest thing to do. As today's demands continue to spiral out of control—be it from family or work or our own unrealistic expectations—we realize that time seldom opens up for us. We must create time for ourselves.

• The most common way that young mothers today find this time is by rising about an hour before the rest of the family...or staying up an extra hour after ever one is asleep. One's own body clock usually determines which will work for you.

• Make time for that weekly exercise or yoga class. Space will not just appear.

• Plan in friends and relatives time on a weekly or monthly basis. Others can nourish our soul.

Unfortunately it seems to be that every new generation learns anew that "youth is often wasted on the young."

Parent Pointers

There are not really lots of things that truly save time when you have a young family. Kids, by their very nature, simply take lots more of your time. But here are a few that do.

Cool It

Keep a small college-sized refrigerator in a baby's room to store the evening and morning bottles and drinks for yourself if you are nursing. This will save you from having to run to the kitchen.

Ready Set Go

Dress your toddler in loose or sweat-type play outfits (versus traditional pajamas) at bedtime. In the morning you just need to change a diaper and you're ready to be off to day care.

Diaper Detail

Have more than one changing area in your home.

Oh Baby

Make a week's worth (or more) of your own baby food in a blender or food processor. Freeze it in molded ice cube trays then store 'cubes' in a freezer plastic bag. Just remove frozen "cubes" as needed.

Be Prepared

Have young children pick out their next day's outfit at bedtime. This can save a lot of morning dawdling time. (Put cold breakfast cereals and bowls on the kitchen table and save yourself time there too.)

Sandwiches by the Loaf

Make a whole loaf of peanut butter lunch sandwiches on the weekend. Wrap them individually and place these back in the bread loaf bag. Store in the freezer. You or your kids can take one out as needed!

Color Code Your Kids

Assign each child a color and let that color determine and organize that child and his or her place in your family. Susie gets the pink towel (so you'll know it is her's on the floor), the pink cup (the one that didn't get into the dishwasher) and the pink scissor, gloves and the like. It will lessen fights and make the obvious, "obvious!"

By the Clock

This may not save you time but it can save you sleep. When you have teens who are old enough to have late curfews, set an alarm clock for the time they are due home. Place it just outside your bedroom. As long as they get home before curfew and turn OFF the alarm, you will not have to waken and check on them. They can't be angry at you...after all it, is the clock they are up against.

Working Parent Sanity Savers

All mom's are busy, but a working mom is twice as busy. Children increase the pressure when you are working. You are running at a breakneck speed from the time you get out of bed in the morning until you fall into bed at night.

As you lay in bed at night you worry about saving enough money to pay off the mortgage, educate your children, put away for retirement and if you remembered to throw Joey's gym suit in the dryer. There are days you wonder where you will find the energy to get out of bed and go to work! How can you do it all? Well, no matter how much you multi task you can't achieve perfect balance everyday in your life. You can however, rethink areas of your life and come up with ways to do some things more efficiently.

Efficient Wardrobe
Simplify getting dressed for work everyday. If you work in an office, wear matching pants, skirts, jackets and sweaters in a neutral color, such as black or navy. You can change your look by adding scarves and jewelry.

Pre-Arranged

Arrange your clothing by category such as blouses, jackets, skirts and dresses, or by purpose—work versus leisure—for example. You can pick out what you want to wear in half the time.

No Time to Iron?

Turn on the shower and hang any wrinkled clothing item in a steamy bathroom area to release wrinkles. The other trick that often works is to just water-mist the wrinkled item on a hanger. By the time you're finished with your make-up, major creases are gone.

A Staggered Commute

One way that you can reduce the time spent in traffic commuting is to ask your employer to arrange alternative work hours. Come in and leave a little earlier or later, in order to avoid traffic congestion.

Electronic Organizers

Electronic organizers (like a BlackBerry, PalmOne, Q or Razr) can help you stay organized and save time but they can also waste time if you do not have the proper one for your needs. Here are a few things to think about before you make a purchase:

- Make sure you can press one key without bumping into the other keys.
- Notice whether or not they respond well to your touch.
- Is it simple to use?

Try the model out at the store to see if you can easily figure out how to update an address or phone number. With some models the procedures for such tasks are far more involved than with others. If it seems to make a simple task more difficult, pass it up. Things will only go down hill from there.

Keep a back up copy of information you can't live without one. Information sometimes can be erased accidentally if it is dropped or comes in contact with water. And sometimes they just get lost!

Bring It On
If your grocer, florist, dry cleaner, or any business you use offers delivery, take advantage of it. The time you save will be worth the cost.

Colored Calendars
Keep track of the family's activities by mounting a large calendar in the kitchen near a box of colored markers. Use a different color marker for each family member. You can then tell at a glance, who is doing what.

Phone Home
Give beepers or cell phones to your on–the–go, never–on–time children so that you can always let them know when to come home or call in.

Automatic Teller Machines
Save time by choosing the least busy hours to visit your ATM. Avoid lunch hours, paydays and generally Thursdays, Fridays and Monday mornings.

Excuse Me
Avoid interrupting yourself. Keep your desk neat and well organized and the things you use the most within easy reach. You can waste as much time searching through a messy desk as you would if someone had stopped in to chat.

Signal the Corps
Close your door halfway or all the way when you do not want to be disturbed. Let your family know that this is your way of saying you do not want to be interrupted—unless it is very important

Rubber Stamp

Save time paying bills by using a rubber stamp with your name and address on it or your signature. You can order rubber stamps at most stationary or office supply stores.

Put Your Back To It

If you can position your desk so that your back is to the entrance of your office, You will be less likely to be distracted by daily office traffic.

Game Files

Don't keep game files on the computer that you use for work. It is too easy to get the irresistible urge to pull up that solitaire file and then spend the next half hour playing games. If you already have them on your computer—delete them NOW. Go off them cold turkey.

In Transit

If you spend a lot of time in transit, a cell phone that handles e-mail can be a time saver. You can handle things as they come up instead of returning to a nightmare of unreturned messages when you get back to the office. .

Speak Up

Ask co–workers to help lighten your load at work. Tell your boss you need more help. When your boss gives you another project and you are still working on something else, ask him or her what you should focus on and let that be your priority.

Give Notice

Let family and other people know that you must complete a project by a certain time. Realizing that other people will be aware of your failure if you don't make the dead line, may be enough to give you the motivation you need to move along.

Laundry Details

Dry Quicker

When drying wet laundry add a few small, clean, dry towels to the dryer load. The whole load will dry faster.

Stash in a Basket

If you always have stacks of clean laundry in your laundry room waiting to be put away, here is a time saving trick for you. Buy a laundry basket for each member of your family and label it. Then when folding the laundry instead of stacking it on top of the table or washer and dryer, place each person's clothes in their basket. This makes it a lot easier for children to put away their own laundry, and your laundry room looks more organized. You can even put their clean socks into a mesh laundry bag and throw it into the basket also. They can mate their own socks. And if you are using my color-coding method for each child (page 17), knowing which socks belong to who is a cinch.

Not Too Fussy?

If you are not too particular about the laundry, you can take the mesh bag idea a step further. Buy two mesh bags for each family member. They can place their colored clothes in one bag and their whites in another. Just throw the entire bags in the washer and dryer. Then hand the bags to the family members to either fold or hang up.

In Between

You know how you are always dropping socks and things in between the washer and dryer and they are hard to remove? If you place a narrow piece of carpet on the floor between the appliances, when something drops you can just pull out the strip of carpet and the article comes with it.

Inside Secret

When folding your linens, place the folded fitted sheet and the pillowcases inside the flat sheet before putting them in the linen closet. This makes finding the right set of sheets a breeze!

Sock It to Me

You resent the time it takes you to match up family members socks? Then don't. Toss clean socks in a plastic shoe-box organizer and let them find their own sock mates.

Simple Solution

Launder everything in cold water. It will save on sorting and avoid shrinkage.

> You may delay but time will not.
>
> — Benjamin Franklin

ZIP THROUGH HOUSEWORK

Have you ever wondered how professional housecleaners cope with cleaning all those dirty houses, day after day? Most cleaning professionals clean at least two homes a day, five days a week. That is a lot of houses! And if you asked them, most would tell you they enjoy it.

To those of you struggling to clean one home this must seem unbelievable. But professional cleaners (of which I am one) know how to go about cleaning. They have ten secrets they use to make the job of cleaning easier. These are things you can apply to your cleaning to get the job done right and in less time.

Secrets Of Professional Housecleaners

Plan On It
Set a day and time. Whether it is cleaning one room or an entire house, schedule a day and set a time limit. That is what the pros do.

Dress For The Occasion

Wear the proper clothes. Most professionals wear uniforms, but you can do just as well by wearing a white blouse (this is important, believe it or not), comfortable slacks and non-slip shoes. You cannot clean house wearing your robe and pajamas. Do your hair and make up before you start. Why? Because you will probably clean a few mirrors and this helps boost your spirits when you see yourself looking good.

Get It Together

Have all your supplies with you. Don't waste time running back and forth getting supplies. Carry them in a cleaning caddy or a small bucket. I have found a favorite bucket where the cleaning caddy fits inside available from Cassabella (www.cassabella.com) or at bed and bath stores. You can carry all the tools and supplies you will need to clean every room in your home.

The Long and the Short of It

Attach an extension cord to your vacuum cleaner so that you can vacuum longer without having to stop and look for another outlet. A minute here and there really adds up.

A Place To Put It

Have containers for trash as well as a basket for items that do not belong in the room you are cleaning that will need to be sorted. That saves you time running from room to room putting things away or making piles that you will have to pick up later.

Professional Method

Use a method. Professionals work left to right, and top to bottom. Thanks to gravity, dust and dirt "fall." You vacuum last, not first. And clean right to left (okay, left to right if you prefer). That way you do not miss anything. Pro's call it "walking the cleaning grid."

What Am I Cleaning?

Identify your dirt. Use the proper cleaning solution for the job you are doing. If you have grease, you need a de–greaser; if you have a hard water build–up, you need a shower cleaner. If you have questions about what cleaner to use, call a janitorial supply store. They are usually happy to help you. You can find them in your yellow pages.

Set Awhile

Let the cleaner do the work. Give your cleaner "dwell time." So many people spray on their cleaner and then immediately start wiping, especially when cleaning kitchens and bathrooms. This uses too much elbow grease. Professional cleaners let the cleaner loosen the dirt before they start scrubbing. And when using antibacterial cleaners, the cleaner needs to set for at least ten minutes or it is not doing any good.

If It Ain't Broke...

If it's clean, don't clean it!

No One Home

Don't answer the phone. Let the answering machine pick it up. And don't make any phone calls either. This will save you loads of time.

What Was I Doing?

Don't let yourself get distracted or detoured to another room until you finish the one you are working in. This is where the sort basket really comes in handy.

Follow these simple rules and you will be cleaning like a pro. Now if you can just figure out a way to get paid like a pro for what you do!

One of the greatest labor saving inventions of today is tomorrow.

Good Cleaning Tools Save Time

Having the right kind of cleaning tools can save you hours of frustration and wasted time. I see people everyday struggling along with vacuum cleaners that don't work and cleaning cloths that are leaving behind more dirt than they are picking up.

Sales of vacuum cleaners are at record levels–but so is customer dissatisfaction. Manufacturers have added a lot of bells and whistles to get your attention and it is working. We now have tools on board with mega amps–some even have built-in air cleaners. A vacuum cleaner is one of the most important tools you have to work with and you should have a good one. Notice I said a good one, not an expensive one.

Suck It Up or How to Pick a Vacuum Cleaner

It is best to purchase your vacuum cleaners at a store that also repairs them. These are the people who know about vacuum cleaners. If you aren't sure which shop is the best, call a maid service in your area and ask them whom they use.

- The more steel parts you have on your vacuum, the longer it will last. Plastic breaks easily. A steel handle and steel beater bar are a must on an up–right vacuum cleaner.
- You should be able to change the belt without an entire tool kit. You can waste a lot of time changing a belt if it is complicated. You should change the belt at least every three months. Even if it is not broken, it stretches and you are not getting the maximum cleaning power.
- Attach an extension cord to your vacuum cleaner to save time. You plug and unplug your vacuum a lot and by using the extension you can vacuum a lot longer without unplugging it. Also, if the plug breaks, you just need to get a new extension cord—not have the plug repaired.

- Having tools on board may seem like a time–saving idea, but I have found that these vacuum cleaners tip over easily, which is frustrating. I recommend having two vacuum cleaners. An up–right and a canister.

Other Tools You Need To Speed Up Cleaning

- A long handle lamb's wool duster for cobwebs.
- A short handled lamb's wool duster for general dusting. I can dust an entire room in five minutes with one of these.
- A pumice stone. An invaluable tool for removing hard water rings especially in toilet bowls.
- A dust mop to spiff up wood and tile floors.
- A squeegee for windows and many mirrored surfaces.
- A cleaning caddy to carry your supplies from room to room.
- Cleaning cloths. 100% cotton for drying-terry cloth are good for scrubbing and something soft like an old diaper for dusting. Microfiber cloths are a good alternative.
- A mop for washing floors (I don't use them) but they can make washing a floor more agreeable to some people.
- A bucket and your choice of cleaning solutions.

There are all kinds of disposable "wipes" on the market that you can purchase—disinfectant wipes, window wipes, dusting wipes, etc. These are quick and easy if you want to spend the money. The mop systems that are on the market can be timesaving too. The important thing to remember is that you do not want to get a build-up of cleaner on your floors. The chore of removing the build-up, will wipe out all the saved time. Mopping your floors once a month with a vinegar/water solution will remove most of the cleaner residue.

> If you think time heals everything,
> try sitting it out in a doctor's office.

Handling the Front Entry

The front entry to your home says a lot about you. It is the first impression that people get of your house and in some cases the only impression.

In my business in which I own a maid service, I personally visit every home before I send my employees to clean. I can tell by looking at the front entry, whether the house is going to take a lot of time to clean or not.

The dead give–aways are:

O the chandelier covered with dust and hanging so high that you would need a 20 foot ladder to clean it.

O the mirrored wall that was installed to make the hall look larger that is so filled with fingerprints I keep looking around for all the people. (And there is usually an area at the top of the mirror that I can tell has not been cleaned since it was put in, because like the chandelier, you can't reach it.)

O the row of family pictures lining the stairs, most of them askew and covered with dust.

O the pile of shoes in the corner that have put black marks on the walls.

O the closet door that isn't shut because there is a backpack blocking it.

O the stack of papers on the bench or table that looks as if it will spill onto the floor any minute.

O a piece of Scotch tape attached to a remnant of a birthday balloon on the door frame.

Does this remind you of your front entry? If so, there is still hope. What's needed is a little planning.

Decorating Tips For Faster Cleaning Of The Front Entry

- A light fixture that is accessible and easy to clean
- Paint on the walls that can be washed repeatedly.
- A small mirror for that last minute check of your appearance.
- A bench for sitting to put on shoes and boots.
- A floor that cannot be damaged by water and cleans easily.

The rest is a matter of storage and decoration.

Hallway Helps

Importance Of Mats
Put a mat at each entrance to your home. Almost 80% of the dirt on floors comes in through the door. A commercial mat is the best. You can purchase these at most janitorial supply stores or warehouse club stores. Stopping dirt at the door saves LOTS of time cleaning floors.

Washable Rugs
Place a rug that can be vacuumed in the front entry in the summer and in the winter replace it with one that can be washed.

Key Holder
An attractive key holder/hanger that works for your lifestyle is essential in the front or back hall. Looking for lost or misplaced keys wastes LOTS of time. Even if you just choose a drawer to hold keys, it will work as long as everyone gets in the habit of putting keys there.

Time Wise
A clock is another must-have in the hall, especially if you have children. Children do not understand time and this helps keep them on track.

Good Hangers

For hallway closets invest in good hangers made out of plastic or wood that will support your coats and jackets without bending under the weight. The thin wire hangers that you get from the cleaners just don't work here. Saves time picking up and re-hanging coats.

Don't Double Up

Put only one coat on each hanger. If you double up coats on a hanger, the one you want will always be underneath and you will waste time removing the outer coat.

Neat Hangers

When you take a coat out of the closet, take out the hanger too. Remove the garment, place the empty hanger on one side of the closet, and push the remaining coats toward the other side. This keeps hangers neat and accessible.

See-Through Containers

Have separate see-through containers for hats and gloves. Less to rummage through and because you can see what's in the containers, it saves grabbing the wrong one.

Safety Pins

Attach a safety pin to your winter gloves and pin them together before putting them in container. Saves time trying to match them up.

Color Code

Color coding hats and gloves works great. Buy each child a different color set of matching hat and mittens. Even the youngest child will have no trouble finding the ones that belong to them.

Shoe Basket
Keep a large basket by the door where everyone can deposit shoes.
This should save time searching for lost sneakers

Mark Shoes
Several people in the household wear the same size sneaker? Use a
permanent marker to mark the inside heel of the shoe. You can use
initials or once again color code to match hats and mittens.

No More Puddles
In the winter place a large plastic laundry basket or boot tray outside
the door in the garage or the mudroom for drippy boots. This is a real
time saver. No more cleaning up puddles.

Removing Boots
Keep a supply of large plastic bags near the place you remove boots.
When you help a child remove his boots, place the boot (containing
the foot) into the plastic bag, and you will have no fear of making a
mess or getting mud on your clothes—or the floor.

School Stuff
Purchase a storage bin or container for each child. Label each with
their name and place on a shelf, in a reach-able location, near the door,
where they enter your home. Have them place their school material
in the containers when they get home from school. This saves a lot of
time looking for lost homework and school bulletins.

Children's Level
Make sure there is a place for children to hang their coats at their level.
A coat rack with hooks works the best for children. You can't expect
them to hang up their coats if they can't reach the hook.

No More Late Fees
Get a see–through bag with a handle where you can put the rented
videos or DVDs that you must return. You can hang the bag on
a hook and when you are done watching the video/DVD place it

in the bag and you will see it as you leave the house. This will be a reminder to bring it back to the video store. No more late fees! No more searching for which titles you're finished with. (Or try *www.NetFlicks* and rent what you want using your computer and your mailbox.)

Save a Trip

If your staircase is working overtime as a closet, shoe rack, toy box, and dumping ground, consider purchasing a Stair Tote. This is an attractive and portable receptacle made of wicker, that is designed to "fit" on 2 stair steps and will hold a variety of items. It won't necessarily save you time, but you'll think it did!

> People who have an hour to kill
> usually spend it with people who don't.

Liberating the Living Room

I am constantly amazed at how much time and money people spend to decorate their living rooms and most of the time it just sits empty. It really is a shame. There are some homes I clean that if the family dog passed away in the living room no one would ever find it because no on goes in that room. And yet we make it look lived in. We put out little dishes of candy and periodicals (Have to have periodicals and journals they speak of our interests.) We also display our collections in this room and that can be a real dust problem. Nothing more embarrassing than having someone pick up your glass frog and seeing the outline delineated on the table.

If your living room looks dirty, even though it is not used, it is probably not dirty, just cluttered.

Decorating For Quicker Cleaning Of The Living Room

- Avoid tufted sofas and chairs. They're real lint catchers.
- Extremely dark or extremely light furniture is going to show lint and dirt.
- Don't accumulate furniture with grooves and ornate moldings.
- Wicker and cane furniture are best avoided as well as elaborate lamp shades. Remember the flatter the surface, the quicker you dust.
- End tables with glass inserts are even worse to clean than glass–only tabletops. There are two different surfaces which requires two different cleaners.

Lambs Eat Dust

Keep all books in a bookcase and dust with a lamb's wool duster. It only takes a few minutes of dusting to prevent dust from building up.

Hide the Television

Television screens attract dust. They do. Having yours in an enclosed cabinet and keeping the doors closed when not in use helps eliminate some of this problem.

Dirty Pictures

Some very nice picture frames are covered with black velvet on the back, making them hard to clean. Use a lint roller, the kind you use on clothes to remove the dust. This is a lot quicker than getting out the vacuum.

Under Foot

Footstools with lift-up lids are a wonderful way to hide those outdated magazines you plan to read...someday.

High Roller

If you have a pet who sheds, keep a lint roller handy for quick clean-up of sofas and chairs.

Pretty Coasters

Have lots of pretty coasters available for your guests. It is a lot easier to wash a coaster than to try and get a water spot off your good table.

Doilies On The Chair

Do you remember your grandmother placing those beautiful hand crocheted doilies on the arms and backs of her furniture? Well, these were not just for decoration. They were there to protect the furniture. People have oil in their hair and dirt on their hands and the doilies prevented the arms and backs of the furniture from becoming soiled. You may not have beautiful doilies but you can accomplish the same thing with a few small linen napkins that match your fabric. They are a lot easier to wash than the doilies.

Furniture Indentations

It is a good idea to move your furniture over just an inch at least once a month, to prevent the legs of the furniture from making indentations in your carpet. But if you have not been doing that, the pile can usually be brought back by placing a damp cloth over the indentation and ironing it. Use a small brush and brush lightly when dry. Be careful not to let the iron touch the carpet. Dropping an ice cube and letting it melt into the indentation is another way to revive a carpet dent.

Who Moved The Cheese?

Placing a piece of cheesecloth or a fabric softener sheet inside your heat vent will prevent dust and dirt from being blown into the air, thus your drapes and furnishings will stay cleaner longer. These should be replaced every three months. This can also be a good way to determine when your furnace needs to be cleaned.

Carved Furniture Crevices

To clean crevices in carved furniture, use a very soft paintbrush sprayed with furniture oil. But remember, carved surfaces increase your cleaning time, so it is far better not to have them in the first place.

Water–soluble

Check to make sure the fabric you choose for your upholstered furniture is water-soluble. Otherwise water spots will stain and it will render any Scotch Guarding you have done less useful.

Painless Plants

Plants add a lot to a room, but choose wisely. Ferns drop leaves, some rubber plants as well as cactus can stain carpet. Small plants that can be taken to the sink and watered are the best. Plastic or ceramic pots work well; clay pots seem to stain the carpet.

People go on vacations to forget things...
and when they get there...they find they have.

Boudoir Bliss

I read the other day that young couples are so busy that they are finding it difficult to find the time and energy to be intimate.
In some of the bedrooms I have encountered, I can certainly understand why. By the time a couple can wade through the piles of clothes to get to the bed and then clear off the bed, who has any energy left?

There is usually a piece of exercise equipment draped with clothes; night stands are filled with used tissues; empty water bottles and sticky lozenges are stuck to the table tops. The lower part of the night stand has open shelves with everything from old socks to stray toys collecting dust.

The floor beside the bed is strewn with books and magazine articles they are trying to read about "Staying In Love" or " How to Loose 50 Pounds in 50 Minutes."

The dresser is covered with loose change, old theatre tickets, receipts and almost-empty bottles of perfume. They can no longer find the chair because it is filled with laundry for the dry cleaners. A television and VCR/DVD will usually set on the end of a table or dresser with all the wires exposed. Tapes will be piled randomly nearby.

And this is where couples go every night to relax! Who can be romantic or relax in this type of atmosphere?

The bedroom has become a "catch-all" room where people shut the door and try to forget about the mess. The bedroom should be a haven for unwinding from the stresses of everyday life. It should be more than just a place to sleep.

You can create a restful and comfortable environment in your bedroom with just a few simple ideas.

Decorating For Easier Cleaning Of The Bedroom

- Buy furniture without curves and ledges where dust can settle. Do not have night stands with open shelves. Make sure everything is enclosed.
- Comforters take the work out of bed making.
- Enclose television and VCR equipment, and keep the units

small, so they do not overwhelm the room. They should not be the focal point of the room. After all, the bedroom is for relaxing!

- No tufted chairs or pillows. (I've said it before and I'll say it again.)
- Make sure you have lots of storage for magazines and reading material.
- Don't get a bed that is too big for the room. You need space to walk around the bed. Never push it up against the wall.
- Shades are better for the windows than blinds. Making the bed creates dust and blinds will collect it all.
- Smooth lamp shades–no pleats, please.

Hanging Out

Hang your clothes in the closet, not out on the exercise equipment. Not only will hanging up and putting away your clothes make the bedroom look a lot cleaner, but it will save you time ultimately. It only takes a few minutes and it is well worth the time and effort. Some of the wrinkles will hang out, so you can save on dry cleaning bills too!

Fast Change Artist

Make your beds up faster by following the hotel-staff style. Hotel beds are made up with two FLAT sheets simultaneously, tucking in both sheets. Then you just fold back the top of the top sheet and you're done.

Shoe Fly Shoe

A hanging shoe holder on the back of a door is a great place for shoes. If you put your shoes away in pairs, you won't end up wearing one black and one brown shoe to the office. Keeps people from looking at you strangely.

Black Belt In Closet Organizing

Installing a "belt" hook will keep your belts in order. But, you must remember to place the belt on the hook. Always a catch, isn't there?

Hats Off

Hat boxes make wonderful storage containers in your bedroom. You can stack them on top of each other for even more storage. I keep one large hat box in my bedroom for stray things I find while cleaning. Then I can put the items away at my leisure.

Magazine Basket

A basket next to the chair is a great place to keep all those magazines you tend to collect. And it looks good also.

Glass Tops

Have pieces of glass cut to fit the tops of your night stands. This will prevent spilled liquids from staining the wood and the resulting time and expense to correct the problem. But if you do spill something, make sure you don't let the water slip between the glass and the table. This can be disastrous to a wood finish if the water is left there.

Coasting Along

Putting small plates or coasters on night stands to hold water glasses or lotion jars will save cleaning time and damage to your tables if you haven't a glass topped table.

Wood vs Carpet

Wood floors in a bedroom are the best especially if you have allergies. You know how often you are likely to move the bed to clean under it. Beds are hard to move on carpet. With wood floors, you can easily slide a dust mop or vacuum under the bed to get those dust bunnies.

Trunk Storage

An attractive trunk at the foot of your bed does double furniture duty. You can sit on it to put on your shoes, and it gives you a place to store extra blankets and pillows.

Tumbling Your Bedspreads And Curtains

To quickly freshen up bedspreads and curtains between seasonal cleanings, place in the dryer with a damp towel and a fabric softener sheet, tumble on the air–only setting for about twenty minutes.

Clean Closet Floors

The easiest way to keep your closet floor clean is NOT to store shoes there. Off–the–floor shoe racks, wall holders, and shoe bags that hang in the closet are good storage options.

Neat Necklaces

Long necklaces and chains have a way of tangling if you keep them in a drawer. Here's a better idea. Install a kitchen utensil rack (the kind sold for ladles, spoons, etc.) on a free wall in the closet and hang your necklaces up. Or use clear push-pin tacks on a near by wall area to hold them.

Dress Up The Dresser

Beautify the dresser with a pretty glass tray or china plate for perfume bottles, cosmetics, jewelry or other small items. This makes dusting the dresser a whole lot quicker.

Long Talk

If there is anywhere you need a cordless phone, it is in the bedroom. I have gotten dressed many a morning while talking on the phone. It's the best way to multi-task. A long cord just doesn't cut it!

Hide And See

If you have an armoire in your bedroom, you can install a mirror on the inside of one of the doors. It is a handy thing for a quick check of yourself and one place hardly anyone will ever see fingerprints!

It's not the hours you put in—it's what you put in the hours.

Bathroom Shortcuts

Ah, the bathroom! The bathroom has changed a lot over the years. The bathrooms are much larger and filled with a lot more stuff. It is not unusual to find five bottles of assorted shampoo and conditioners, three or four kinds of toothpaste, all sorts of creams and lotions, plus all the electrical equipment we take for granted, such as hair dryers, curling irons, shavers, toothbrushes etc. Sometimes it takes ten minutes just to put away all the items on the counter so we can begin to clean it.

The bathroom used to be purely a functional room. Now it is more like a showplace. People have added everything from telephones to exercise machines to their bath areas. The showers and tubs are so much bigger and, alas, create more mildew.

You can save a lot of cleaning time in a bathroom by choosing the right kind of tile, counter tops, etc. Here are fifteen things you can do when remodeling or building a bathroom to make it quicker to clean.

For Speedier Cleaning Of The Bathroom

- Don't let the bathroom technicians talk you into a lot of unneeded accessories. A giant whirlpool sounds great, but will you really have the time to use it? We have found that most people usually take a shower.
- Avoid fancy art in the bathroom.
- Make sure the tub and sink are deep and have wide rims. Less splashes on the floor.
- Stay away from dark colors for sinks, tubs and toilets. Hard water marks show on dark surfaces.
- The new showers without doors are great! No curtains or glass doors to clean.
- You lose valuable storage space with pedestal sinks.
- Use enclosed lighting to protect fixtures from hair spray and dust.
- Large tiles cut down on grout area. Mid-tones show dirt less. No dark colors, please.
- If possible, install wall mounted toilets. This eliminates cleaning a toilet base.
- Never carpet a bathroom floor. Area rugs of washable size are all you need.
- No mini-blinds please, especially dark colored ones, in a bathroom.
- The mirror should not come all the way down to the counter or it will gets lots of splash marks.
- Buy bathroom wastebaskets that are smooth inside and easily washable. They have some beautiful baskets on the market but a lot of them are not practical. You can waste a lot of time cleaning gum out of a wicker basket.
- A good (preferably enamel) washable paint on the walls is a must.
- No grooves, pits or ornate handles or faucets. More work for you and less time for the things you really enjoy doing. Crystal-type handles, on the other hand, show no marks.
- Avoid MARBLE in the bathroom. Marble requires care, unless you are the type of person who will wipe up every

drop of water as it hits the counter or floor. Marble is a soft stone and is hard to keep clean. Fortunately many tiles simulate marble today.

Just when you think tomorrow will never come, it's yesterday.

Coming Attractions
Attach a magnetic strip to the back of the medicine chest door to hold tweezers, clippers and other small metal objects.

Hang Ups
Limited space? The more you can hang or store, the easier it is to keep counters clear for quick cleaning. Hang a shoe bag on the back of the bathroom door to store hairbrushes, curlers, extra washcloths, etc.

Handy Cleaning
Always keep a basket or bucket with the cleaning supplies you use to clean the bathroom underneath the sink. Then you are always ready for a quick spiff-up.

Slick Idea
Apply a little baby oil or furniture polish to your glass shower doors after you clean them the next time you take a shower. The soap and water will bead up and run off making cleaning the shower easier the next time around.

Fast Track
To clean the track of a sliding glass shower door, first wet down the track with white distilled vinegar. Use a small screwdriver wrapped in a thin towel to pry loose the stubborn dirt. An old toothbrush works well also.

Shower the Shower

Running the hot water for five minutes before scrubbing the shower will loosen up the dirt and grime and make bathroom cleaning faster.

Bathroom No–No

Don't store shampoos and conditioners on tub corners or shower floors. Instead place them in a portable caddy hooked over the shower head. You will have less surface to clean and those surfaces will clean up faster and easier.

Squeegee In The Nude

If you will train yourself and your family to squeegee down the glass areas each time they shower, you will never get a hard water build up. Buy a large squeegee to make it go faster.

Leave It Open

After you shower leave the glass shower doors open, or the shower curtain depending on what you have. This lets the air circulate and helps prevent mildew.

Shower Curtains

Buy cheap vinyl liners for your shower curtains. When they become mildewed, just toss them out and get a new one. The liners can be washed but why bother.

Rub–A–Tub Tub

Bubble baths are fun but they do leave a residue that makes the tub harder to clean out. Let the water drain out of the tub while you are still in it, then take a small sponge or wash cloth and wipe the line of residue from the tub. Turn the water on and rinse yourself and the tub and you're done.

Standing Orders

Sometimes the easiest way to clean a tub is with a floor sponge mop dedicated to only that purpose. It's fast and lots easier on your back.

Oil's Well That Ends Well

Putting a little bath oil in your bath water is a great help cleaning the tub. Nothing sticks to the tub, the residue wipes right out. Take care, however, as it can make the tub slippery.

Weighty Problem

When purchasing a bathroom scale, think smooth. Most of the time they have slip proof rubber tops and those get filled with dust and hair spray—making it another item to keep clean. If you already have this kind, store it under your bed and slide it out when you decide to weigh yourself. I don't know why manufacturers make them like that. I have never heard of anyone who has gotten hurt falling off a scale, have you?

Hairy Scary

Vacuum your bathroom before washing the floor and there will be less to wash. Get in the habit of vacuuming the sink area to remove hair too. Otherwise clean hair out of the sink using some toilet paper or a Kleenex rather than a sponge when doing just a quick clean-up.

Hair Spray Haze

To quickly remove hair spray from the bathroom mirror, clean it with rubbing alcohol. It also works on your chrome fixtures.

Brush Your Sink

Use an old toothbrush to clean around and behind bathroom faucets. Removing this residue each week saves a lot of time in the long run.

Pickled Porcelain

If you have a hard water build-up problem in your bathroom sink and around the faucets, you can saturate a paper towel with white vinegar and apply it to those surfaces. Let it set for several hours. While it is soaking you can be off doing something else. Phosphoric acid will also do the trick quickly but is not as easily obtainable.

Hooked On Hooks

Make sure you have plenty of hooks in the bathroom to hang up the wet towels. There are some great over-the-door hooks that work quite well for this purpose. You don't want to waste time picking up the family's wet towels. And let them know that.

Dry on High

Your hair dryer can be used to quickly clear a steamy bathroom mirror, dry underarms or dry stockings that you forgot to wash until the last minute.

On Hold

Store extra toilet paper rolls somewhere in the bathroom. They can even be spooled on a decorative plunger behind the toilet. How many times have you been interrupted with the call "Will you bring me some toilet paper?" No one seems to notice until they sit down. Save yourself some steps.

The best way to kill time is to get busy and work it to death.

Kitchen Management

At the seminars that I present, I ask the question "Which two rooms in your house are the hardest to keep clean?' The answer is always the same—the kitchen and bathroom. We spend more time in the kitchen than any other room in the house. Over the years we have made a lot of changes to our kitchens. We have installed radios, televisions and computers. It is a virtual media center. Why go to any other room in your home when you have it all in the kitchen? I would not be surprised to see some sort of bed in the kitchen in a few years. Then we would each have a "bed & breakfast" in our own home. Not!

The following is a list of some of the clutter I have seen in a kitchen:

O Dry cleaning hanging from the light fixture.

O Old tires leaning against a wall.

O Refrigerators so covered with magnets and notes that you could not find the handle.

O A broken television with the children's school pictures glued to the screen.

O Two refrigerators side by side. (Do not confuse this with a side-by-side refrigerator.) This was two separate refrigerators, one working, one broken. No one bothered to remove the broken one.

O Four large dog dishes on the kitchen floor, in a house where they had no dog.

Remember, it is not usually the dirt in your kitchen that visitors will remember, but the dirty dishes in the sink and all the clutter on your counters and table.

Decorating For Quicker Cleaning Of The Kitchen

- Think "smooth" when purchasing items for your kitchen. Grease abounds in this room and will settle in every tiny crevice. The only exception to this rule is the outside of a refrigerator. In this case 'rough' is better because it hides fingerprints.
- NO appliances made of stainless steel. OK, I knew you would not like that one but I have cleaned enough kitchens with stainless appliances to know how time consuming it can be to keep them looking nice.
- No dark colored appliances (especially black)
- No chairs or tables with lots of spindles and places for dirt to collect.
- Recessed lighting is a must! It will save hours of cleaning time.
- Smooth cooking tops are great! No drip pans and grates to clean.
- Floor covering should be neutral in color, easy to wash and scratch-resistant.
- The walls should have a paint that can take a good scrubbing.
- Counter tops should be smooth and a neutral color.

Just following a few of these suggestions, when choosing items for your home, will save you hours of cleaning time.

The Junk Drawer?...Yes, the Junk Drawer

First, let's talk about junk drawers for a minute. I know this is not a subject that most people talk about. In fact, I know a few people that will not even admit to having one in their home. Why? They are embarrassed. To admit you have a junk drawer is to admit that there is a place in your home that is not neat. And not only that, it is a place that you allow disorganization. No one wants to be thought of as disorganized. So, they just don't talk about it.

Home builders never ask you "Where should we install the junk drawer?" Remodeling experts just pretend they don't exist. Cleaning experts (such as myself) seldom mention them. Even people who have no qualms about discussing the details of their latest operation at the dinner table seem to shy away from bringing up the junk drawer.

But, let's face it, everyone has one! Some people have more than one. This is the place where you put the unidentifiable objects such as screws and keys just in case they turn out to be important. And no junk drawer is complete without an assortment of pens and pencils that don't work. A few coins, a roll of tape, a golf ball or two and you have yourself a junk drawer. I found a golf ball in my junk drawer last week, and I don't even play golf! The junk drawer is a homeless shelter for stray items and a fast way to clean off your counter or desk.

Junk drawers play an important part in the management of households. We all need at least one place to put things and not feel as if we must keep them neat. Having a junk drawer does not label you a disorganized person, and as long as it is a drawer—and not a room—it has probably saved you some time along the way. (A drawer takes less time to toss or de-clutter than a room.)

I am only going to give you one tip regarding your junk drawer. Talk about your junk drawer with a friend and I am sure you will quickly realize that you are no more disorganized than the next person.

Tools

Boxes Versus Baskets
A lot of people like to use baskets for storage in their kitchen. I recommend using containers with lids in this area. You have to deal

with a lot of grease and moisture in this room and lids keep items cleaner and safer. Beware of "organizers" that are actually space wasters that take up twice as much room as the contents they're meant to hold. Spice racks are a good example.

Multi-Tiered Food Storage Shelves
A handy way to store your spices for quick and easy access is to purchase the small stair–step type storage shelves. Many have three levels for storing spices and other small containers. Some will expand to fit various cupboard widths. Larger sizes may be available for storing bigger containers such as cans and olive oil. Don't confuse these containers with "spice racks." Unlike spice racks, these containers are easy to clean.

Food Clips
Plastic clips that snap shut and look sort of like hair barrettes are great for fastening opened bags. Keep a bunch handy in your kitchen for quickly closing bags of frozen vegetables, nuts, etc. Actually heavy-duty office clips work well too.

Here are some additional time–saving tools that you may wish to consider:
- Rice Cooker
- Crock Pot *(You can throw something in it in the morning and come home to the smell of delicious food cooking. I love mine.)*
- Large Pasta Pot with a colander insert
- Vegetable Steamer: My daughter almost wears one out in the summer time when fresh vegetables are so readily available.
- Salad Shooter *(I have never owned one, but some of my friends swear by them.)*
- Universal Measuring Cups
- Toaster Oven
- Small Electric Food Processor *(I use this a lot because I live alone and make small amounts of things.)*

- Parchment Paper *(This is great for lining cookie sheets, a little expensive, but worth the cost I think. It's a trade-off to cleaning cookie sheets.)*
- Electric Knife which is especially good at Thanksgiving and Christmas.
- Food Thermometers *(These help you save time trying to decide when food is done. Especially good for meats.)*
- Gravy Separator/ Pitcher
- Coffee Grinder for grinding seeds, nuts, grains and coffee.
- Universal pot cover — a pot lid designed to top all pots in your kitchen.

Detergent Dispenser With A Brush

Save an extra step by dispensing soap as you scrub. Some dispensers may work better for you than others. See if you can buy one at a store where the staff has tried the product.

Long Handled Bottle Brush

This cleaning tool is great for cleaning crevices of jars and bottles. It also works well if you're trying to get your brush in close around the inside bottom edges of pots and pans.

And may I suggest that you get your family to help, especially your children. You will be surprised how rewarding and time saving it can be. Even very small children can help to mix batters and set and clear the table. You also get the added benefit of time spent together. And with all this help and time saving tools, maybe you can try twitching your nose and disappear from the kitchen all together! Alakazam!!

Enjoy yourself. These are the good old days
you are going to miss in ten years.

51

Kitchen Cleaning & Organizing

Ready, Set — Clean
Keep a plastic basket under the sink containing the following: Small dustpan, squeegee, de-greaser, window cleaner, small brush, scrubby and a box of baking soda.

Presoak Power
Clean as you cook. Keep the sink (or at least a bowl) filled with soapy water so you can soak utensils or pots and pans as you use them.

Johnny-on-the-Spot
Wipe up spills and drips right away. A quick wipe will save you a scrubbing session later.

Soak Before You Scrub
Always let hardened spots soak with water or cleaner before you start to scrub. It saves elbow grease as well as your time.

Read All About It
Spread some newspaper or paper towels on the counter when you are cutting flowers or doing other messy jobs. When finished, just roll them up and throw it all away. You can buy throw-away paper cutting boards which are great, if you don't mind spending the extra money. Or save on paper by keeping an old phone book around and tear out pages to use for messy, throw-away jobs.

Squeegee It Up
Drop an egg on the floor? No problem. Keep a small dust-pan and a squeegee under the sink for quick pick ups. This works better than a paper towel. A baster to suck up the raw egg is another choice.

Bigger Pots

Make sure you use big enough pots to cook your food. You will have less spatters that way.

Spatter Screens

Spatter screens are also great for covering pots to prevent spattering. These are readily available at department stores and some grocery stores. Another good alternative is to buy pots with see-through glass tops.

Pumice For Oven Spots

Pie spill over in the oven? Now you have a big black spot to remove? Grab your pumice stone. Not the one you use on your body, but the one designed for porcelain and toilets. Wet the end of it and rub your spot away. It saves cleaning the entire oven. (Not to be used on self-cleaning or continuous cleaning ovens, however).

It's In The Bag

For a quick clean of drip pans and oven grates, spray them with oven cleaner and seal them in a large plastic garbage bag overnight. Next morning just rinse, clean and dry. So easy!

Blender Blues

Dirty blender? Fill with warm water; add a few drops of detergent; and turn on for a few seconds. Rinse and drain dry.

Boil Your Troubles Away

Scorched pan? Don't panic. Just fill the pan halfway with water and add 1/4 to 1/2 cup baking soda. Simmer awhile until the burned portions loosen and float to the top.

Grungy Teakettles

To remove lime deposits in kettles, fill with equal parts vinegar and water. Bring to a boil. Remove from the heat and allow the kettle to stand overnight. Rinse clean.

China Stains
To remove coffee and tea stains from fine china, rub with a damp cloth dipped in baking soda.

Drain, No? Drain, Yes.
Clogged drain? Pour a cup of baking soda followed by a cup of vinegar down the drain...let mixture foam, then run hot water. Repeat as needed.

Grater Ease
For a fast and simple clean up of your hand grater, rub or spray salad oil on your grater before using it.

Line'r Up
- Line your crock-pot first with an oven-roasting bag before putting the ingredients in.
- Line your cookie sheet with disposable parchment baking sheets.
- Line the bottom of a baking dish with aluminum foil when using a recipe that is messy.
- Line the bottom of a freshly cleaned microwave oven with a piece of waxed paper.

Bag Trick
Store a few extra trash bags underneath the one in use in your trash container. The next time you take out the garbage, there will be another liner ready to go.

Don't Stick to It
When using ingredients such as honey or peanut butter, spray the measuring cup first with a nonstick spray or oil. It makes cleaning the cup much easier.

Pre Pam Pans

To reduce time spent scrubbing roasting pans, you can also spray them with a nonstick spray whether the recipe calls for it or not.

Gone Fishy

After frying fish or onions put ¼ cup of vinegar in the pan. Cover and cook slowly for 10 minutes. Pour out vinegar and wash the pan in hot soapy water and there will be no odor.

Clean Cut

Which cutting board is best—wood or plastic? From the studies I have seen, it is just a matter of preference. Germs linger on plastic longer but it is easier to wash off than wood. Which ever you choose, make sure you clean it well after each use, especially after cutting raw meat.

Order of the Day

When unloading the dishwasher, always remove items in relation to the cabinet in which they are stored. For instance, all the glasses first, then the plates. Makes sense, doesn't it?

Avoid Dishes Altogether

Think disposable. Use coffee filters for serving hot dogs on a bun, wrap sandwiches, for lining a bowl filled with popcorn or even a dip. Toothpicks are utensils beloved by kids in place of silverware. Occasional diet drinks are a meal in a disposable can. Use a flat bottom cone to serve tuna salad, cottage cheese or for baking a dessert in—and, yes, even for serving ice cream. And of course there are paper plates!

Don't Sweat The Small Stuff

When loading a large load of dishes into the dishwasher, always start with the small items first. If you run out of room, it is much easier to hand wash a few large items than a lot of small ones.

Wax Eloquent

Place a piece of waxed paper on the bottom refrigerator shelf if you have open shelves. This will save you some cleaning time. Of course, the paper should be changed frequently but this is a lot easier than trying to remove the dried Kool-Aid from the bottom of the refrigerator.

Caddy Shack

Get in the habit of storing freezer items in plastic caddy trays. In case of a power failure, food items will only drip into the tray or plastic holder and clean up will be manageable.

Open Sesame

For a quick clean of your can opener, run a piece of damp paper towel through it once or twice.

Coffee á Go-Go

A thermos bottle is easy to clean if it is freshly used, but let it sit underneath your car seat for a week or two and it is a different story. If freshly used whether it is made of glass, stainless steel, or plastic, just rinse with a solution of dish soap and hot water. Rinse well and store with the cup and stopper removed to prevent odors and bacteria growth.

To clean the ones with dried on residue, fill the bottle with hot water and a few tablespoons of baking soda. Allow it to soak overnight. If the odor is a problem, soak in a solution of hot water and lemon juice. Never put a thermos bottle in the dishwasher. And avoid immersing the entire bottle in water since water could seep between the bottle and the insulating liner.

Coffee Maker Caretaking

I want to tell you to clean your filter basket and glass carafe each day. This would go along way in preventing the stains that occur on coffee makers. But I know most of you won't do that. I have seen coffee makers that looked as if they had not been cleaned in years. For some reason, coffee makers don't get much attention. I can tell you that simple baking soda will remove those stains! Wash parts in hot soapy water and then sprinkle the inside with baking soda and scrub away the stains. Rinse and you are good for another week or two.

The brewing mechanism should be cleaned about once a month to prevent the mineral deposits from building up and ruining your coffee maker. To do this, just pour 2 cups of white vinegar into the carafe, then fill to the 10 cup level with cold water. Pour the mixture into the water reservoir just like you were going to make a pot of coffee. Place a fresh filter in the basket and turn on the machine. When about half of the mixture has brewed into the carafe, turn the machine off and let it set for 20 minutes. Pour the mixture back into the reservoir and brew it all this time. Before making coffee again brew a pot of plain water. Do this procedure while doing other routines in the kitchen so that it is not a separate event. It will make your coffee maker last a long time. And your coffee will taste better for it!

A No-wash Resting Place

Use a piece of waxed paper, foil or a sponge as a spoon rest. Nothing to wash.

Garbage In, Garbage Out

To prevent disposal buildup, grind only small amounts of waste at a time. Do not put waste in the disposal without running it. About once a week fill the sink with warm soapy water and 1/2 cup baking soda. Turn on the disposal and pull out the stopper. This will help eliminate odors. Grinding citrus peels is also good for odors. Occasionally grind ice cubes to break up grease deposits on rotors.

Always use cold water when running your disposal. Easy things like these will prevent big problems.

Labels Front and Center & Other Sticky Stuff

Removing those stickers and tape residue can be a real challenge. But it wouldn't be if you did not put them on there in the first place! Get yourself a nice size piece of magnetic board—about 18" by 18." Place this on the refrigerator door and then place your photos and reminders there! You can remove the whole board for cleaning and no more sticky door problems. But if you need to remove some sticky stuff before you do this, soak a cloth in warm vinegar and apply to the sticky area or any decal there. Hold it there for a few minutes until the area is saturated. It should peel off easily.

Minimize Mildew

Wipe down your refrigerator occasionally with white vinegar—especially the area around the doors. This will prevent a bigger cleaning problem later on.

If You're Not Frost-free...

The next time you defrost your freezer, try spraying nonstick cooking spray on the ceiling and the side walls when finished. Any ice that forms will slide off next time you defrost.

Tip Top Ways

That awkward cupboard above the refrigerator may serve you better if you take off the doors and install vertical dividers. Now you have a place for cutting boards, trays, cook books, cookie sheets, etc.

From Broom To Room

Fill your broom closet with shelves to create a pantry (or a linen closet). It will hold lots more than an unshelved closet. Hang your brooms on the back of the door. And it's faster to access.

Recipe Clippings

Store recipes you find in newspapers and magazines in a big envelope taped to the inside cover of your cookbook. At the very least, use a sturdy file folder with a closing cover that stays with your cookbooks. Store these items and your most used cookbooks on a shelf in a kitchen where they are easy to get to. Extra cookbooks not frequently used could be stored in other bookshelves in another room.

Shine On

If you spray the top of your stainless steel stove with Liquid Gold or some other kind of oil polish, spills will clean up quickly. It also will make it shine like new! The same procedure works on stainless steel refrigerators and dishwashers.

Baby Your Faucets

Every once in awhile wipe your kitchen faucets down with baby oil. This will make them shine like new and protect them from hard water build-up.

Managing in Like-Minded Ways

Keep milk, cheese, juices, etc. in the same place in your refrigerator so you won't waste time looking for them. Do the same for pantry staples.

Hold That Thought

Group together those skinny packets of powdered salad dressings or soft-drink mixes in a plastic cherry tomato or strawberry box, or small see-through plastic container.

After purchasing grocery items such as flour, sugars, cereals etc., place them in see-through containers, too. Not only does it keep them safe from bugs but you can always tell at a glance what you are running low on.

Keep from Jamming

Use decorative tins to store drawer "snaggers" like cookie cutters, cake decorating supplies and other odd shaped gadgets.

Hang It Up

Keep measuring spoons in easy reach by hanging them from cup hooks inside the door where you keep your spices.

Box Your Bags

Those plastic bags from the supermarket are too good to use just once but they tend to get out-of-hand fast when you just shove them under the sink or put them in a drawer. Correct this mess quickly by placing them into an empty tissue box or a cool tote that hangs on an out-of-the-way doorknob. Stuff the bags in and pull them out one by one as you need them. (Or recycle these at a local, environmentally-friendly food store.)

Kitchen Cemetery

This is the area underneath your kitchen sink where you store all the dead cleaners that you bought that do not work. Weed out anything you do not use and put the rest into a square dish pan or some other kind of container. Do not store anything under your kitchen sink that is not placed into a container. This makes cleaning so much easier. Plus if any of these containers leak, the mess is confined to the pan holding the cleaners.

Time-out In the Kitchen

Every kitchen needs a timer—and not for timing food when it is baking. You need it for shortening those phone calls! You know how it is. You get home from work, you are trying to get dinner on the table and everyone you know seems to call you! With the timer, you place it near the phone, set it for three minutes. When it goes off, you can easily say "Oops, my cake *(pasta, cookies, etc.)* is done, can I call you later?" You will be amazed at how much time you can gain by doing this!

Grocery Shopping Time Bytes

We all love to eat, but if you are like me you hate to grocery shop. I have found that delegating that task to another family member saves a lot of time but if you are stuck doing the task, here are a few ideas to speed it up.

List It
Keep a list on the refrigerator door or near the phone, to keep track of any groceries that run out. An attached pen/pencil doesn't hurt either.

Organize That List
Before you shop, organize your list, group products from each area of the supermarket (like dairy products and meats) together. You will fly through the aisles. Actually make yourself a master list on your computer to work from. Put a fresh one up after each trip to the store.

Highlight It
After you have written your grocery list, use a high lighter pen to mark items for which you have coupons so you'll be sure to get the right sizes.

Coupon Time Savers
If you are a coupon saver, organize your coupons in the order of the grocery aisles. This will allow you to save time and money because you will be able to find the coupons you need when you need them. Did you know that you can print out coupons on the Internet for stores in your area? (See page 94.)

Shop Off Times
Try to do your shopping at "off" times. Early mornings or late in the evening the stores are less crowded and easier to cruise through.

Saturdays and Sundays are busiest and often have less selection by late in the day.

Chill Out

When unpacking groceries, put all refrigerated items together next to the refrigerator so you open the door just once.

Shop Alone

If you can leave your children and spouse at home, you'll probably find shopping faster, easier and less expensive. Each additional person shopping with you increases the temptation to buy on impulse.

Leave It to Beaver...or Anyone Else

If your area has a grocery delivery service such as *Simon Delivers*, use it! It is not much more expensive than a regular grocery store, and you will save lots of time as well as money because you won't be tempted to buy those extra impulse items. Let's face it, how many times do you actually get just what is on your list. Try it. You might really like it.

> If you want to leave footprints in the sands of time,
> you'd better wear work shoes.

Food Fundamentals

Some days don't you wish you could be like the "Genie" and twinkle your nose and dinner would be ready? I think we all feel like that at times. We would like to speed up the chopping, dicing, peeling and mixing that it takes to prepare a meal. Well, I can't give you any magical solutions but here are a few kitchen tools that will speed the process up for you.

Time Saving Tools

Garlic Peeler
The type generally referred to is a rubber tube you place the garlic in, roll it a couple of times and the skin comes off. An added benefit: No more garlic smell on your hands.

Anything Dishwasher Safe
Check for the magic time-saving words "dishwasher safe" before purchasing any item! Don't buy anything you have to wash by hand until you check to see if there's a comparable dishwasher–safe item from another company.

Flexible Plastic Cutting Board
Flexible plastic cutting boards are favorites with many people. After cutting vegetables, fruits or herbs, you can lift them up and pour contents into whatever bowl or pan you're using. They are even dishwasher safe!

Own More Than One Cutting Board
Avoid cross–contamination when cutting different types of foods for the same meal by owning several cutting boards. This is especially important if you're cutting raw meats, poultry or seafood and then need to cut ready–to–eat foods. With more than one cutting board you can avoid spending extra time washing your board before cutting the next item.

Pump Spray Or Mist Spray Bottle For Oil
Fill this non-aerosol sprayer with your favorite oil and use for flavoring vegetables, coating pans and grills or spraying directly on bread. (Buy a container specifically advertised for use with oil.) Glass bottles are easier to clean.

A Good Quality, Sharp Chef's Knife
This tool is a must in any cook's kitchen. Use a chef's knife to quickly chop, cut, slice, dice and mince fresh produce. You can do procedures faster with a chef's knife than with a food processor and easier to clean up. It's important to keep your knife sharp. Check what type of sharpening procedure or device the manufacturer of your knives recommends.

Food Processor and Blender

A food processor can make quick work of slicing, dicing, shredding, grating and chopping...especially for large quantities of food. For smaller quantities, hand held kitchen tools such as chef's knife or a grater sometimes are faster.

A blender makes quick work of pureeing ingredients, such as soups, and is terrific for making smoothies! Buy a heavy-duty blender if you want to crush ice. Some people like a hand held immersion blender for pureeing soups in the pot or frothing hot chocolate.

Colander Collection

If you tend to wash and /or drain a lot of foods for meals, an extra colander or two may save you time and help prevent cross–contamination. Place one on a plate after rinsing some fruits (blueberries, etc.) and save yourself the time of cleaning another bowl.

Kitchen Shears

Sturdy, sharp kitchen shears can perform many tasks—from cutting herbs, bacon and pizza to trimming dough, de-boning chicken and cutting poultry joints. Many are labeled dishwasher safe and will separate for more thorough cleaning. As with any sharp items, use caution. If you wash shears in your dishwasher, place them in a location where they won't bump against other items or cut someone.

Apple Corer/Wedger

Use this tool to quickly core and separate apples and pears into wedges. You can also buy just an apple corer. Great trick for avoiding waste when giving a child an apple to eat.

An Assortment of Whisks

A whisk can be your quick and clever companion in many food adventures. Match the size and shape of your whisk to the task. A big, rigid whisk for foods in large pots; a medium whisk for soups, creams and custards: and a small whisk (about 10 inches long) for salad dressings, sauces and folding flour into batter. Some whisks are longer and narrower, others are like big balloons. Use the "balloon-ingest" ones when you want to beat a lot of air into a mix, such as whipped cream or meringue. Choose whisks with thin and flexible wires for whipping air into batters, and thicker, more rigid wires for thicker mixtures such as brownies. Choose ones that have the area sealed where the wires go into the handle. This helps assure your whisk stays clean. These whisks may be more expensive, but will probably last longer and cost less over time. Look for "dish-washer" safe tools to save time and to help assure they are thoroughly and safely washed.

Microwave-safe Glass Batter Bowls/Mixing Cups
Use these multi-purpose tools to measure; mix (batters, sauces and toppings); cook foods in the microwave; and reheat foods you want to pour, such as soups. Many come with plastic covers so you can use them for storage also.

A Good Quality Vegetable Peeler
Quickly and evenly remove the outer skin from fruits and vegetables with a sharp, durable vegetable peeler. Many have a sharp, rounded edge at the end to pop out the eyes of the potato.

A Digital Timer
Help keep your kitchen tasks under control with this battery-operated device. Time the exact seconds, minutes or hours needed for a cooking process. Many come with a flip-out stand and a magnetic backing, so you always can keep them handy. Some can be clipped to your belt if you need to leave the kitchen. Others come with a string to hang around your neck.

Kitchen Tools With Ergonomic Rubber Handles
Many cooks find these special-handled tools are easier on their

hands, particularly if they use a certain tool, such as a vegetable peeler, for extended periods.

A Set of Scoop Measuring Cups

For items such as sugar, oatmeal, rice, etc., quickly scoop the amount you need. Some scoop type cups are a cross between a scoop and a regular measuring cup. They have a long handle attached to a base. (Note: You wouldn't "scoop" flour for most recipes. To avoid packing, it's usually advisable to measure flour by spooning it lightly into your measuring cup.) Regardless of your preferred type of measuring cup, you may wish to own at least two sets to save clean–up time between different uses.

Cookie Dropper

If you bake lots of cookies, use this tool to make more uniform cookies in less time than you can by dropping dough from a spoon. Cookie droppers look like mini ice cream scoops where you push the lever on the handle to push out the dough into baking pans. You can also use a vegetable non-stick spray on the droppers for extra easy use.

Funnels

Kitchen funnels are helpful for transferring bulk items into smaller containers. One cook ground a week's worth of coffee, put it in a jar and stored it in the cupboard. The rest of the beans went into the freezer. If you transfer ground coffee to a smaller coffee container, a funnel is handy. It's also great for filling sugar shakers from a larger package of sugar.

Salad Spinner

If you're washing lettuce, spinach leaves, etc. on a regular basis, this tool is a must. Simply toss in your washed greens and "spin" them dry. These products work in various ways. Some have knobs you turn. Others separate through a push down mechanism. Check around to find the one with features you like.

Multi-functional Baking Dishes and Mixing Bowls

Save cupboard space and cleaning time by purchasing baking dishes suitable for baking, microwaving and storing food. Likewise, purchase microwave/oven safe mixing bowls suitable for storage and attractive enough to set on the table.

Non—stick Skillets With Sloping Sides

This item helps you cook with a very small amount of oil, and clean-up is quick! The sloping sides makes it easy to turn and remove food. To protect the nonstick surface, use spatulas and stirring spoons made for use with this type of non-scratch coating.

Heat-resistant Spoon-shaped Spatulas

Mix, scrape and stir again at the stove with this utensil. Once you try these, you may want them in several sizes.

Narrow Spatulas

Use this utensil to scrape out the last bit of food from the nooks and crannies of jars.

Jar Opener

If your only jar opener is a flat piece of rubber or you don't have an opener at all, check out the kitchen gadget section at your favorite store. Some of the latest models let you stick the jar lid between two prongs and twist. If you're tired of holding jars under hot water, hitting lids on the counter or giving up and reaching for a different food, this may be the tool for you.

Cheese Slicer

If you eat a lot of cheese, this tool makes quick work of slicing a block of cheese. But if buy your cheese already sliced (like I do) you will not need it.

And, of course, **A MICROWAVE** oven! *(I didn't really forget.)*

Meal Time Management

According to the studies that have been done, most people have no idea what they are going to have for dinner until about 45 minutes before mealtime. You know how it goes. You are on the way home from work or the kid's soccer game and all you can think about is how hungry you are and what are you going to make for dinner. Sometimes you end up with more people for dinner than you expected. Don't be caught empty-handed.

With these basic ingredients in your pantry and you will always be ready for whatever comes your way.

A Stable of Staples

Pasta: It tastes great in soups and casseroles or you can toss it with meat, left over chicken and vegetables.

Cream of Mushroom Soup: This is an ideal base for quick casseroles. Thin with milk or wine for a tasty fish or poultry sauce.

Rice: It is used to feed the world, so why not use it to feed your guests? Wonderful as a base for casseroles, fried rice, vegetables, etc. Just add canned meat, fish or any leftovers.

Instant Mashed Potatoes: A great side dish. I used to dislike instant potatoes, but I found that you can doctor them up with butter, chicken broth and milk and they are great!

Canned Tuna, Chicken, Salmon And Shrimp: You can whip up a lot of things in a hurry with these magic cans.

Tomato Sauce: A jiffy starter sauce for spaghetti or pizza. Mix it with canned beans for chili, or use as a soup base.

Frozen Green Beans/Peas: For a speedy side dish, defrost, drain and toss with herbs. Great for stretching a casserole or just added in tossed salads.

Instant Boxed Puddings: Kids love these and they are so quick to make. Top with a little whip cream and you have a dessert fit for a queen.

Powdered or Frozen Drink Mixes: Better for the kids than soda pop and can become a punch by just adding a little ginger ale or carbonated lemon drink

Ground Beef: You can make so many dishes with ground beef. I buy large packages and divide it up into one pound size containers and keep in the freezer. Or freeze it "flatten" and it will cook up in no time.

Also when you are cooking ground beef you can cook several pounds at once and freeze it cooked Then when you need a pound of ground beef all you have to do is thaw.

Canned Fruit: You can chill a few cans for dessert or mix with some whip cream for a great fruit salad.

Canned Mushrooms: These can be used to liven up frozen pizza and added to all kinds of casseroles.

In two days, tomorrow will be yesterday.

Cooks' Quick Tricks

There are many little shortcuts that you can incorporate into your favorite recipes and meal preparation. Here are some you might not be aware of.

Hole In One
When making up your own hamburgers patties, shape them like a doughnut with a small hole in the middle. They will cook faster that way.

Hot Tip
Chunks of meat on a metal skewer cook more quickly when in the oven, in a broiler or on an outdoor grill.

Cook Once; Eat Twice

It doesn't take that much more time to prepare a double of any recipe. Cook it in one dish or two, and put one away for future use.

Half Time Game

Cooking chicken or meat on a grill? Precook food about half way in your microwave, and then complete it on the grill. Or the reverse. Foods started (and seasoned) on a grill can be finished up in the microwave oven to shorten cooking time.

Basting A Turkey

Drape a few strips of bacon over your roasting turkey to baste it automatically.

Whipping It Up

Let egg whites stand at room temperature before beating. They will fluff up faster.

Olé

For a fast pie crust, use a flour tortilla as a bottom crust. Cut a second tortilla in strips for a criss-cross top crust.

Cabbage Shortcut

When making cabbage rolls, instead of softening the cabbage leaves in boiling water, just freeze the entire head of cabbage first. When thawed the leaves will be soft and ready to use.

Chop Chop

Next time you have your food processor out, chop up a few extra onions and store these in a plastic bag in your freezer. Just take out what you need when a recipe requires you to first sauté chopped onions.

Slicer Dicer

Cut up small cooked potatoes for potato salad quickly using a hard-cooked egg slicer. It also works on mushrooms.

It's In the BAG

Reduce washing dishes by mixing various fixings in a closed one-gallon plastic bag instead of a bowl. Or just put each hand into a plastic sandwich bag to mix anything that is messy which would make hand clean-up a chore.
- Hamburger/meat loaf
- Cookie dough
- Bread dough
- A marinade
- Dry ingredients
- Salad fixin's (For a crowd, use a larger plastic garbage bag. When ready to serve, toss in dressing and put in a serving bowl.)

Cut Ups

Use your pizza cutter to remove crusts from bread, cube bread for croutons, cut up sandwiches, dice small greens and herbs, cut spaghetti into child-size bites, and, yes, even serve up pizzas.

Un, Deux, Trois

Pick up a cookbook that has recipes using only 3 to 5 ingredients.

One thing we know about the speed of light
– it gets here too early in the morning.

Breakfasts Briefs

Eating breakfast is one of the best things that you can do for yourself and your family. Studies indicate that people who eat breakfast have better problem solving skills, memory, attention span and even physical work capabilities than those who skip breakfast.

So, take the time to eat breakfast to provide energy and speed up the rest of your day. It doesn't have to be complicated to be nourishing. Here are a few suggestions:

- Low sugar, high-fiber ready–to–eat cereal topped with sliced banana and yogurt.
- Peanut butter on bagel or toast with milk.
- Yogurt sprinkled with whole grain cereal.
- Bran muffins served with fresh fruit. (Frozen muffins are perfect for microwaving.)
- Breakfast shakes can be made with milk or yogurt, fruit and a teaspoon of bran.
- Instant hot cereals.

Peanut Butter Crisp
Microwave one tablespoon of peanut butter for 30 seconds. Drizzle over one cup of fiber cereal. Top with one medium sliced banana.

Jamming
Spread your favorite jam between two pancakes for a Breakfast Jam Sandwich. You don't have to cook up fresh pancakes. Toast ones from your freezer—homemade or store bought.

English Muffin Pizza
Put your favorite cheese and a spoonful of spaghetti sauce on top of an English muffin and microwave for about 30-40 seconds.

Cuppy Cheese

Melt some cheese in a coffee mug and serve it up with a spoon or bread sticks.

Egged On

Hard cook 6 to 12 eggs at a time and store in the refrigerator. There is nothing faster than a hard-cooked egg for breakfast. Not a bad snack either!

Lickety-split Lunches

Lunch is another fast food meal for most of us. We often combine our lunchtime with catching up on errands. We end up eating lunch in the car while on the run. In fact the U.S.-based National Restaurant Association says that 63% of American workers skip lunch once or twice a week, 55% do something other than eat during their lunch hours, and 40% cut back on lunch in order to keep up with their increasing work loads.

Here are a few fast things to keep on hand for those days when you need the energy but won't or can't make time to eat:
- Granola or energy bars.
- Packages of crackers and cheese (or peanut butter).
- Small packages of nuts—bought or repackaged by you.
- Fresh easy-to-eat fruit such as bananas, apples, pears and plums.
- Cheese sticks.
- Bottles of water.

If you have a little extra time, try one of these:

Almond Tuna

Tuna fish boring? Doesn't have to be. Mix in tuna-onion-celery-mayonnaise and slivered almonds. Serve on whole grain bread. Delicious and crunchy!

Black Bean Chili

Makes enough to last for a few days. Brown one pound of hamburger, drain and put into a large pot. Add 2 cans of drained whole kernel corn, 2 cans of drained black beans, 1 can (14 oz) diced tomatoes, 3 tsps. of chili powder and 2 tsps. of cumin. Add a little salt and pepper and one cup of water. Cook for 15 minutes. Serve with garlic toast or crackers. Makes enough to last for a few days. Put some in a thermos or a small container that you can reheat and take it with you to work.

Betty Burgers

Brown one pound of ground beef in a medium skillet. Drain the meat. Return to skillet and add one can chicken and rice soup, 4 Tbsps. of catsup, 3 Tbsps of brown sugar, 1 one tsp. of French's mustard. Simmer for 10 minutes. Serve on hamburger buns with potato chips.

Hearty Soup

To create an extra hearty soup, add some canned corn to your favorite canned soups, such as clam chowder or cream of tomato.

Tuscan Dish

Add canned white beans to your favorite tomato sauce. Then toss with fanciful cooked pasta for a true Tuscan course.

Dinner Dealings

Dinner is the time that hopefully you and your family get a chance to sit down to a nutritious meal and catch up on the day. But with soccer, basketball and meetings it too is sometimes a rushed affair. The faster that you can get a meal on the table, the better chance you have of spending some quality time with them. Buying frozen entrees are the answer for many. There are a lot of very good ones on the market. Some of them I even prefer over what "Mama" used to make.

And if you are picking up one ready-to-eat meal, pick up a second one you can put in the freezer and save yourself a trip. Even if it's just a pizza.

Today's timely trick is to combine pick-up ready-to-eat food favorites with a few choice items you cook up yourself for a quick meal for you, your family or even when there's company.

With just a little extra effort you can make the dishes below to add to your repertoire:

Meddling with Meat Loaf

For a Mediterranean meat loaf, add sliced canned olives to your regular meat or turkey loaf recipe. Then top with a sauce of diced canned tomatoes or half a bottle of chili sauce.

Choice Three Bean Salad

Mix canned red, black and green beans with a garlic vinaigrette and a dash of chili powder for a spicy, southwest "ready-to-eat-with-any-meal" three-bean salad. Or the traditional three bean salad of a can of green beans, yellow beans, and red beans in a marinade of 1 cup sugar, ½ cup vinegar (plain white or fancy flavor) and 1 cup of vegetable oil. To this you can always add yellow beans, garbanzo beans and thinly sliced onions. Store in the refrigerator.

Fast and Fishy

Place fish fillets in a glass-baking dish. Sprinkle with salt and pepper. Pour lemon juice or cooking wine over the fillets. Cook at 400 degrees for 10 minutes, then turn down to 350 degrees and continue cooking until done or about 15 minutes. Or place the baking dish (appropriately covered) in your microwave for 7-15 minutes, depending how many are pieces in the dish.

Hamburger Stroganoff

Sauté ½ cup minced onion and 1 clove minced garlic in one tablespoon of butter. Add 1 pound of browned and drained crumbled hamburger, plus 2 tablespoons of flour, salt and ¼ tsp. pepper plus 1 can (8 oz) of canned drained mushrooms. Cook for 5 minutes then stir in 1 can cream of chicken soup and simmer for 10 minutes. Add 1 cup of sour cream and heat through. Serve over egg noodles or rice.

Chicken Gourmet

Cut up, store-roasted chickens (aka rotisserie chickens) are perfect when adding a little "creativity" before reheating and serving.
- Cover with a cup (or small jar) of apricot preserves and a cup of orange juice. (This can easily be prepared the night or two before you plan on serving it.)
- Cover with a can of Coke (no substitutes, please) before reheating in the oven.
- Use one straight from the store for a "pulled" chicken dish.
- Make a chicken Caesar salad or chicken salad of your choice or use the following one.

Chicken Salad

For a quick salad, combine chunks of rotisserie chicken (left over from the night before?) with drained, canned mandarin oranges and pineapple chunks. Dress the salad with mayonnaise thinned with Dijon mustard and the reserved canned mandarin orange juice.

Fast Finishes

Dessert is always the best part of the meal for me. And it's nice to be able to whip up a quick dessert for those unexpected guests. If you keep a supply of cookies and ice cream on hand, you will always be ready for what ever happens. Some of the cookies you can buy now are so tasty no one will ever know they are not from your oven. And many of the refrigerator cookie logs (just slice and bake) are great. However, if you get the urge to be 'Susie Homemaker" the following recipes are so fast and easy to make, you'll be making them all the time, even if you are not in a hurry.

Quick Cobbler

Pour a can of your favorite pie filling such as cherry or blueberry into a flat baking dish. Heat 10 minutes in preheated oven at 425 degrees. Top with a can of refrigerated biscuits. Sprinkle with a little sugar and nutmeg and bake for another 20 minutes. Serve warm with cream or ice cream.

Banana Pudding

Mix and cook one large box of Jell-O vanilla pudding according to directions. Layer this in a deep bowl with sliced bananas and crushed graham crackers (which you can also buy already crushed in a box). This is so easy your children can do it.

Pear-fect Sorbet

A quick, elegant, light dessert for family or friends. Freeze one can of pears until firm and then puree in a food processor. Serve immediately. A great summer dessert.

Fresh Baked Beauty

Mix one box of white cake mix with ½ cup butter together. Put half of the mixture into the bottom of a square baking pan. Pour one can of fruit pie filing (I'm partial to cherry) over the top of this mixture. Sprinkle the remaining cake mix on top. Bake at 350 degrees for 20–30 minutes. Top each serving with a scoop of ice cream if you have some in the freezer.

No Gripe Grapes

Sweeten 1 cup of sour cream with ½ cup of brown sugar, blending well. Toss with 6 cups of seedless grapes that have been washed and stemmed and chill before serving.

Just a Trifle

Cook one package of vanilla pudding according to directions. Whip one pint of whipping cream (or use approximately 1 cup of aerosol whipped cream) and save a half cup of the whipped pint. Wash and drain one pint of berries (any kind). Mix cooled pudding with whipped cream. Slice a pound cake into 10 slices. (Frozen pound cakes are always good to have in your freezer.) Layer the cake, fruit and pudding in a glass bowl. Repeat two to three times. Top with reserved whip cream.

Snap Crackle Pop

Make crispy rice cereal bars using a jar of marshmallow cream instead of melting marshmallows and butter. Then you have no pot to clean. No extra butter is needed here except for your hands when you press the mixture into the pan. (Easier yet if you mix it all together in a disposable aluminum pan.) If you're a purist and like to make these the traditional way, you can shorten the cooking and cleaning process by putting the marshmallows and the butter in a plastic bowl that has first been coated with a non-stick vegetable spray. Microwave about 30-45 seconds and add cereal. Mix with a spatula that has also been given a non-stick vegetable spray. Mix ingredients and transfer them into a dish which has also been given a non-stick vegetable spray coating. Easy to make—eat—and clean-up.

Don't feel guilty about using fast, frozen or prepared foods or even having food delivered to feed your family. It is more important to be able to sit, talk and eat (however the food makes it to your table) with your family than it is for you to stress yourself out trying to make a meal when there isn't much available time. They will enjoy you more. And family time is precious.

> Nothing is all wrong. Even a clock
> that has stopped running is right twice a day.

Party Hardy

Parties can be a lot of work! When you work outside the home this is even more of a challenge. Sure, you watch television shows on entertaining and dream of being able to set a gorgeous table like they do but let's be real, they have a lot of people helping them.

To be able to plan a great party you need to remember what a party is really about. It is not about what a great cook you are or showing off your house or your creativity. It is about joining together with family and friends to celebrate special moments and creating fond memories.

Here are a few tips and recipes that I hope will make your party planning a breeze and make you look like a catering pro.

Change-A-Date

Try to plan your parties to give yourself more time to recover and enjoy celebrating, For example, move a late December birthday to a different time of year. Give a Christmas party that is NOT just before Christmas.

Do-It-Yourself Omelette Brunch Party

Here's a unique weekend brunch that is easy on you and fun for company. Put each person's name, using a permanent marker, on a freezer-friendly quart zipper-closing plastic bag. Into each bag have your company put two cracked eggs (no shells, please). Close and shake well. From a table or counter that has omelette "fixings" (pieces of green pepper, mushrooms, tomatoes, shredded cheese, cooked bacon, chives, salsa, etc), let each person added any or all of the above. Seal bag and place each one into a pot of boiling water and boil for exactly 13 minutes. A good size pot can hold about 6 bags. (If only cooking 2 bags, submerge for only 8-9 minutes.) Open and the omelette slides right out onto that person's dish. You have few dishes to clean and your company has lots to talk about!

Meals on Wheels

Some places will deliver a complete cooked meal to your door or you can pick one up at a restaurant or grocery store. How easy is that? All you have to do is set the table and clean-up. And who knows? Maybe you will even get some paid help in that department! *(I give you permission.)*

Bring It On

Have all your guests bring their favorite food so everyone contributes some of their time and you don't have to give all of yours. Make sure you tell the guests it is to be already prepared and in a serving dish. Don't be afraid to have them tell you what they want to bring so you have some control. (You don't want someone showing up with a bag of lettuce and vegetables that you have to chop.) Keep a list of all the dishes they will be bringing, so you will not end up missing an important part of the meal. Apple pie is great but twelve apple pies is a little much. Crock-pots are another issue. I was once at a party where nearly everyone brought something in a crock-pot. The hostess was going nuts trying to find enough outlets.

To Clean Or Not To Clean?

If your house is in decent shape, don't bother doing a big cleaning before company comes. There will be plenty of cleaning to be done once they leave. However if you insist on cleaning it, do it three or four days ahead of time. You want to be able to enjoy your guests and you cannot if you are exhausted from cleaning in places they will probably never look anyway. Some folks like having two parties back to back to take advantage of the house being cleaned once and excess food is usually not an issue.

Table Preparation

Whether you are having a sit-down dinner for 6 or a buffet for 30, set your table the day before. Just getting this much done will put you in a party mood and make you less stressed.

Paint Your Wagon

I am always amazed at how people go crazy at holidays re-doing their house. I hear it all the time. (We have company coming. I need to paint the living room and get a new sofa, or I hope the new carpet can be put in before Christmas.) Why? So you can be a nervous wreck worrying about guests spilling things on it? Your life will be a whole lot easier if you don't start huge re–decorating projects before holidays and parties. You are busy enough without the stress of re-modeling. And repeat after me—*this party is not about showing off my house.*

Host Help

If you are planning a very large gathering, get a friend to help you host so that you can enjoy the event. I have a client who has a large Halloween party every year. She hires me to greet the guests, take their coats and the food dishes they have brought. Did you ever notice how several people seem to arrive at a party at the same time? When this happens, it is hard to greet them properly. I also keep an eye on the food and drink tables, and let her know if something is running low. All she has to do is have a good time and enjoy the party, which is the way it should be.

Be a Paper Tiger

There are so many beautiful paper plates and plastic utensils available now that anyone who uses the real china and silverware has only himself or herself to blame if they have to wash dishes. You don't have to do it just because Mom did. However if you enjoy setting an elaborate table, go ahead. It should be fun.

Trash

Have plenty of places for the guests to put their trash. You would be amazed at what you can turn into a garbage container. Large cardboard boxes lined with plastic liners, even large old flowerpots can become attractive trash holders. Or hang a trash bag on a hook on a tree when having a yard party.

Hang It All

If your party is small and you plan to have guests hang their coats in the front closet, make sure you have plenty of sturdy hangers. Or you or they will spend time picking coats up off the floor.

Help Yourself

Meals served buffet–style are perhaps the easiest on you as a way to entertain a large crowd. This is especially true if you are short on seating space.

Head Start

Anything you can do ahead of time helps to simplify parties. Plan foods that can be prepared ahead of time and stored in the freezer or refrigerated for a day or two without sacrificing taste. The best recipe my daughter says I ever gave her, was one for do–ahead mashed potatoes. It was always such a hassle peeling and mashing the potatoes right before the meal. Now she makes them the day before and her life is much easier.

Make Ahead Mashed Potatoes

8-9 large potatoes, peeled, boiled and mashed
2 3 oz. cream cheese packages (or 1 6 oz.)
1 cup sour cream
2 Tbps. butter
1 tsp. salt
2 tsps. onion salt
¼ tsp. pepper
   parsley flakes as a topping prior to baking
Refrigerate prior to baking. Combine and bake at 350 degrees for 30-45 minutes prior to serving.

Big Lots

For large parties, you might want to shop at club or membership stores. You can find large size bags of nuts, chips, gallons of pickles, all under one roof. And the prices are great also. Saves time running from store to store. Here's my favorite large party salad recipe from items easily available from a club store.

Centennial Chicken Salad

2 ½ cups cooked and cooled rosamarina macaroni
5 cups cubed cooked chicken
Cover these two with a mixture of:
2 tsps. salt, 1 tsp grated orange peel, ¼ cup orange juice, ¼ cup oil, ¼ cup vinegar Refrigerate 4 hours or overnight.
Also combine the following:
1 quart mayonnaise, ½ cup chicken stock and 1-2 tsps curry powder and chill at the same time.
Before serving add:
3 cans (11oz. each) of mandarin oranges drained, 2 cans (20 oz. each) of drained pineapple chunks cut-up, 2 cups seedless green grapes, and 3 cups cut-up celery.

Add fruits and celery to chicken/macaroni mixture and toss lightly with mayonnaise mixture.

Place in a large serving dish and sprinke with toasted almonds. Makes 25-30 servings.

Rent A Party
If you don't have enough serving dishes, chairs or other party equipment, think about renting them. It's less of a hassle to get the items you need from a rental store than to try and borrow them. You can get everything you need and most rental places will deliver and pick up for a small fee. Talk about a time saver!

Bar None
It is a lot easier to serve a special drink, such as punch or ice tea, wine or champagne than it is to offer individual drinks. You can

make or chill the beverages ahead of time and everyone can serve themselves. Less work for you.

Fill 'em Up
Go for the party drink mixes you can buy. Some even come frozen and ready to go, such as marguritas. People are often willing to try a drink when there are batches of them so don't worry if you are only offering limited options.

Counter Productive
Line your kitchen counter with a sheet of freezer wrap papers. When all is said and done, just wrap it all up and your clean-up time disappears.

Clean-up
If you can wait until the next day to do the after party clean-up, do so. Take care of the necessary things like putting the extra food away and soaking pots and pans. If you have spots on the carpet, get to those right away. Spots turn into stains that take longer to remove. As for the rest of the clean-up, LEAVE IT! You will have more energy the next day. Sit back and reflect on what a great party you gave and think about the next one!

> The real problem of your leisure
> is how to keep other people from using it.

Technology
To The
Rescue

If you had told me just a few years ago, that I would be writing about saving time with technology, I would have laughed. I was one of those people who refused to get a computer. Computers were toys for the younger generation. I thought it would be too much work to learn how to operate it. It took me a while to master the basics of my computer, but now, I wonder how I ever got along without it!

Once I overcame my fear of computers, I found myself purchasing a cell phone, a scanner, and all sorts of technical equipment. I am so excited about the time I am saving with these new tools.

I have heard people say that technology has made more work for them—especially cell phones and e-mail. They have a difficult time keeping up with it all. But I think this is because they have let their high tech toys become time bandits. These products are not the enemy. They were invented to make routine tasks easier and to simplify our lives. They will do just that if you use them properly. You need to remember that you are in charge of your time. The world won't end if you turn off your cell phone. In fact you might find that your food may digest better. I am by no means a high tech consultant but here are some ways you can use technology to save you a lot of time.

Phones at Your Service

Just Leave a Message
Use the answering machine or voice mail system to screen calls during dinner, meetings, work sessions or family time—then return the calls at your convenience.

You can also leave messages for yourself by calling home to remind yourself of an event, item or chore that must get done.

Caller ID
Caller ID can be an excellent tool to screen incoming calls so you don't waste time talking to telemarketers…or even a friend or relative you simply can't chat with at that moment.

List It
Take time to add your frequently used contacts into your cell phone's calling list. It's pricey these days to call Information/411. Even when using a land line, your cell phone's address list can act as your personal calling directory. With preprogrammed numbers and speed dial on your cell or any phone, you will think you are in heaven.

ICE
ICE is the 'name' to list in your cell phone directory. It means "In Case of Emergency." Should you be in an accident, paramedics and others are now trained to look for this number in your cell phone. If you haven't done so before, list a person who should be called "in case of emergency" now.

Heads Up
Buy a headset for your mobile phone. This is a comfortable way to conduct phone calls and have your hands free. (Caution: talking while driving, hands-free or not, can be a serious distraction.)

A Rainy Day?
Stick to the subject you are calling about. You can waste a lot of valuable time discussing the weather or other minor pleasantries.

Yakkity Yak
Need to call a "talker?" Place your call when the "talker" isn't likely to keep you on the phone or just before lunch or quitting time. Or leave a voice message when you suspect that person will not be there.

Phone Tag
Write a script in case you get an answering machine or voice mail, which is quite likely these days. Remember to leave your name, affiliation if appropriate, phone and reason for your call and the best time to call you back. (Say your name at the beginning of the massage and repeat it at the end.) People are a lot more likely to get back to you quickly if you do this.

Murphy's Law
"Any task expands to fill the time allowed for it." If you plan to make fifteen phone calls and schedule two hours for this, it will probably take the full two hours. However if you schedule only forty-five minutes to make the calls, you are more likely to complete the calls in a shorter period of time.

Finding It
If you forget a contact name, you can spend a lot of time looking for that number. You can avoid this by cross–indexing your address directory by company or service, and also by name.

Phone Projects

Keep a small project by the phone so you can work while you are waiting on hold. Speaker phones save a lot of time. When I am put on hold I just turn on the speaker and go about my business until I hear someone pick up.

Foiling Telemarketers

I understand the service they perform but they really cut into my time. Some ways to avoid this problem are:
- Screen for their calls on your caller ID.
- Ask for their home number so you can 'call' them.
- For callers who say they will save you money, tell them you don't want to save money. In fact, insist that you don't. They seldom have a comeback for that.
- Tell them you don't make pledges over the phone but they are welcome to send you any materials they like. As most are on a commission, they usually hang up.

Strictly Business

Let's Get Together

Telephone conference calls can save time and money. No traveling, food or lodging expenses, plus you save the travel time. You can bring together people from several locations that may not ordinarily be able to meet. Even family members.

Red Carpet Treatment

Keep a VIP list of the more important people you often call near the phone. Include the names of assistants, secretaries and anything pertinent you might know about them. You can make quite an impression by remembering a secretary's name.

Early Calls

People are more likely to be in their offices first thing in the morning. A good time to call is between eight a.m. and eleven a.m.

Bouncing Back

Too busy to talk? If you are engrossed in a task and the phone interrupts, take a second to write down a few key words before you answer the call. Then you will be able to pick up where you left off.

Getting Back

If you are returning a business call, make the person who answers the phone aware of this fact. It will expedite your call.

Straight On

Dial direct if you can. Find out the direct line or extension for the party you are calling. Avoid going through an office operator, if possible.

Computers Savvy

As I have limped into the information age, these are some of the things that I have learned to do that have saved me a great deal of time. You are probably aware of most of them, but there may be a few surprises.

You can keep your bookkeeping, correspondence, financial records and much more on your computer.

Don't be List-less

If lists work for you, let your computer be your friend. Use your computer program-of-choice to keep forms (aka templates) available from grocery shopping lists to to-do lists to computer calendars.

E-Mail Bits & Bytes

E-mail is remarkable because you can have incredibly "small" contact conversations without being impolite. A traditional phone call to the same person would require, by our customs, a much longer interaction.

Once your address book is set up on your computer, you can e–mail anything from vacation plans to new baby news to everyone with a click of your mouse.

If you're away, e-mail allows you to have any incoming mail give an automatic response as to when a person can expect to hear back from you.

Keep in touch with your friends via e–mail. E–mail has made keeping in touch with those far and NEAR so easy and inexpensive.

PINS, Passwords and More

The growing number of passwords and e-mail addresses required of you by different sites seems to grow daily. The problem is that my mind hasn't. They all seem to require different parameters (some want more than 8 characters; letters and numbers, or upper and lower case letters, etc.) which I can't commit to memory. Thanks to the computer, we don't have to. Create a small text file or separate data file you can keep on your computer's 'desktop' that will alphabetize these for you. Just enter the site name, type in your user name and password in any field and save. That's all. This will save you time by no longer asking the site to resend you your access information. (I also save credit card info, frequent flyer mileage account numbers and any other items I seem to need for online shopping.) You can go online and search for password management systems with downloadable programs if your needs are more complicated.

Clean-up the Junk

When you forward e–mail make sure you clean up the "junk transmission" information at the top and bottom of the e–mail you are sending. People don't want to have to scroll down a bunch of old information to get to the good part. This saves other people time.

Contact Info

Place your information in every reply, including address, phone number and extension. This makes it quicker to reach you. Figure out how your system does the 'automatic' signature and get in the habit of using it on all your e-mails.

Beware of Bogus Bugs

Don't waste time worrying about virus alerts and other safety messages from friends that often are a hoax. To check them out go to websites such as *www.urbanlegends.about.com* or *www.snopes.com*. I almost deleted a very important part of my software due to an e–mail of this sort.

Attachments

I have found that it is best to send documents as attachments that can be printed out, as well as copying the text into the e–mail. Not everyone has the same software as you or can open your attachments. Be sure to let the reader know which software you use and what to do if they can't open it. I have wasted a lot of time trying to open attachments that were not compatible with my software. Some friends can open one downloaded photo but not several when in a zip file.

Keyboard Shortcuts

Most commands on a computer can be done in more than one way but usually the fastest are those using the keyboard shortcuts. You don't have to learn them all but if you can learn 2-6 of them you'll speed up your computer time. *(For instance, copy selected text—*

Ctrl + C; cut selected text—Ctrl + X; paste selected text—Ctrl + V; save a document—Ctrl + S; print a document—Ctrl + P.)

Laptop Efficiency

Use two battery packs for mobile laptop efficiency. While one is charging, you can use the other one freely, knowing that a fresh pack will be there when you need it.

The Internet

Book a Book...or a Movie

Get to know the library's online ordering system and save drive time. You can find any title the library carries for books, movies, CD's, or books on tape. Order it and have it delivered to the branch closest to you—all for free. You can also renew your selections when needed online. Now isn't that a time saver?

Shopping Online

Buy ANYTHING online these days. Amazon.com and Barnes & Noble.com are strongest in books and CDs. Compare prices too. Shop competitively for any item (type in item and 'best price' in a search engine or try *www.cairo.com*) and you'll find an array of prices from different places, including some that do not charge tax or shipping.

Catch A Flick

For many theaters you can purchase your movie tickets online. There is a small fee for this service, but it is worth it if there is a new movie you want to see. Beats standing in line for hours.

Buy Stamps

You can buy your postage stamps online too. You can use a program to print them out or have stamps delivered to your door (*www.stamps.com*). No more lines at the post office. (You can also just call 1-800-STAMP-24 with credit card information for stamps that will be delivered.)

Coupon Collectors

Get free coupons online. There are several coupon websites. Just visit coupon sites and enter your zip code. All the stores in your area will come up on the screen. Choose which store you plan to shop at in the next week, then print out the coupons. No more searching through the Sunday paper.

Secure Banking

Do your banking and bill paying online, even if you choose only half your accounts. Sign-up is easy, and what a convenience! Check with your bank about the procedures. You'll have to deposit money the old fashioned way...unless your pay check can be electronically deposited.

Information Please

Quick access to white and yellow pages can help you get needed phones numbers...and at no extra charge. (*www.whitepages.com; www.yellowpages.com*)

Getcha Boarding Passes Here

Flying somewhere? Apart from booking your flight you can check yourself onto your flight from your computer. You can usually print your boarding passes out anywhere from 2 to 24 hrs hours before departure. You can also check weather and the status of departures and arrivals—all on your airlines web site

A Few Uncomplicated Tech Tips

• Get the fastest connection available to you. A DSL or cable modem hookup (if available and affordable) offers download speeds up to thirty times faster than dial-up.

• Shutting down your computer at night is a good way to save energy, but it's no way to save time. The sleep/hibernation feature avoids the slowdown of exiting your computer. (Unfortunately, not every computer can sleep/hibernate.)

• Trying to move a slow mouse around the screen can drag you down. Find the panel that changes the mouse control and increase your speed.

• Get rid of Spam. Use whatever programs are available to you. Deleting these time-wasters is a black hole.

• Avoid instant messaging. It's just one more interruption.

If you want to search the net there are a lot of search engines available to you, and you can waste a lot of time searching them. I like *http://dogpile.com.* It is a search engine that searches a number of the Web's best search engines simultaneously, returning the top ten results from each one.

Later, Alligator

Forward to your evening online address (or save for later) jokes, games and personal e-mail rather than letting it distract you from what you need to get done.

File and Retrieve

For easy filing and retrieval, create one e-mail per subject. This can speed things up a lot as you can search old e-mails by the subject line.

Lost Subjects

When responding to a question or a specific issue, refer to that item in your response. You can't assume the person will remember the topic. You will get a response faster. Some systems automatically copy the e-mail you received; others require you to highlight the information for it to show up in your response.

Photo Finish

You can send digital pictures to your family and friends and now you don't even need to invest in a digital camera! The camera store where you have your film developed can turn ordinary film into digital images for you and put them on a CD so you can load them into your computer. No more running to the post office to mail pictures.

Digital camera companies have worked hard to make it easy for you to download images into your computer and e-mail them to interested (and dis-interested) parties.

Take images (even a short video) by aiming the camera at yourself at arm's length. You will be surprised how well these come out and you don't have to take the time to find someone else who will 'film' you.

Album Keepsakes

You can automatically view and organize your digital photos with a photo album and image organizer on your computer. Visit *expressAlbum.com* or *www.shutterfly.com* for such information. They have several programs that help you quickly organize your photos. Apple computers come with iPhoto for this purpose.

Or upload your photos to an Internet photo digital service (such as *Snapfish.com* or *Otophoto.com*) that allows friends and family to see ALL your photos from a trip, party or family event. They can order their own copies if they wish some.

> Yesterday is experience, tomorrow is hope;
> today is getting from one to the other.

Getting From Here to There

Car Care

Traffic research proves that switching lanes doesn't significantly reduce driving time. The lesson here: pick a lane and stay put. And you'll get better gas mileage too.

Luxury Can be Necessity
If you can afford leather car seats, keep in mind that they take less time to clean up than fabric ones.

Don't Fill 'em Up
While it is best to fill up your gas tank to avoid extra stops, on occasion driving into a full service station with $5 or $10 to hand to the attendant will give you a fast fix when that gauge is looking dangerously low.

Roll-on In
A lint roller is a quick way of coping with crumbs on fabric seats.

I Hear You

No time to read? Get into the habit of listening to books on tape. (Or rather CDs these days.) Your best selection can come from your local library or online services which will deliver to your mail box.

Carting Keys

We all seem to have a lot of car keys these days and they all look alike. In order to be able to tell them apart easily, put something colorful on each person's key ring. Then Dad will have no excuse for leaving the house with Mom's car keys in his pocket. How many times has this happened?

Grocery Helper

Keep a laundry basket in your trunk and then when you purchase groceries you can bring them into the house, a basket at a time. Saves steps too.

Have a Spare

Keep a spare box in your trunk to hold items in need of repair, return, etc. At least it will be in the car (rather than being forgotten)—if you get in the habit of bringing such items out to the car—even if the errand is not yet planned.

Come Fly With Me

We all know how long the lines can be at the airport and how frustrating it can be. But there are a few things you can do to speed things up.

Check It

Curb side check–in is the greatest! You get your boarding pass and your bags taken care of all at once (if you've not already done so at home).

Flight Cancelled?

This usually means a long line for re-booking at the airport. To avoid this problem, find a pay phone or use your cell phone and call the airline's toll–free reservation number to book the next flight out.

Cutting It Close

If you are on a connecting flight and the first leg of your flight is arriving late, ask your flight attendant to alert your connecting gate–and try to relax.

Connection Missed

If it is the airlines fault that you missed your connection, you don't have to wait for your carrier's next flight. Under "Rule 240", you can request an earlier flight on another carrier. You will need to explain why you must get to your destination without delay.
If you are held over more than several hours, you can also request a meal voucher and a free telephone call. Of course the best time saver is to take nonstop flights.

Delayed By Weather

Fewer thunderstorms occur early in the day, so flying early is a wise choice. Never book the last flight of the day if it is cancelled, you are out of luck.

Delaying Yourself

With the time it takes to go through security clearance these days, avoid things that will slow you down. Minimize or avoid metal items or jewelry on your person. Wear shoes that are easy to take off and put on. Don't carry knitting needles, small scissors, small jack knives or lighters.

Who Does It Belong To?

Place identification tags in and on all your baggage. Don't forget to tag your laptop computer. On your checked luggage place some colored yarn so that you can readily identify your bags on the carrousel. It is amazing how many bags look alike.

We are always complaining that our days are too few and acting as though there will be no end to them.

Index

Scharlet Ward has owned and operated Domestic Engineering Inc, a professional maid service since 1973.

Schar was born and raised on a small farm in Linn, Missouri. She credits her mother with instilling in her an early passion for cleaning.

At the age of twenty-one, she married and moved with her husband to St. Paul, MN where she acquired a job as a house cleaner. Her meticulous cleaning services soon put her in demand so she started a small cleaning business. Within a short time her business had grown to the point that she was employing several people and was a growing corporation.

Schar used her hands-on experience to write a helpful cleaning book, COMING CLEAN, eventually published by Book Peddlers. She also began doing cleaning workshops for women's groups.

To add some entertainment value to her presentations, Schar invented an alter-ego, Clara Klutz, to create a humorous opening for those speeches and workshops. Clara, dressed an a scrub lady, played the guitar, shares jokes with the audience and works her act with her daughter Debra Varin. They have traveled all over the Midwest giving entertaining seminars about house cleaning...and now time-saving tips.

Schar has presented seminars at the Minneapolis Home and Garden Show as well as in St. Louis, Kansas City and Peoria, IL. She has done a 20-city TV satellite tour as a spokesperson for Murphy Oil Soap and appeared on the popular Texas TV Debra Duncan Show as well as on SMART SOLUTIONS (HGTV).

Schar Ward lives in St. Paul, MN.